# JoJo
## A Dog's Tale
### An Autobiography

By JoJo Donahue

# JoJo
## A Dog's Tale
### An Autobiography

Copyright © 2008 by Sande Donahue
Copyright © 2008 by Banbury Publishing
Cover art copyright © 2008 by Banbury Publishing

*All rights reserved*

No part of this publication may be reproduced in whole or in part, or stored in a retrieval system, or transmitted in any form or by any means, electronic, mechanical, photocopying, recording, or otherwise, without written permission of the publisher.

ISBN 978-0-9706007-8-3

Printed in the U.S.A.

To the
United Yorkie Rescue Foundation
For being the angels that you are and
bringing our little JoJo into our lives
www.unitedyorkierescue.org

To
Dr. Kim Ogden, Dr. P.H.
Animal Communicator
For her understanding, compassion,
love and invaluable expertise
www.kimogden.com

To
Skip Haynes
Laurel Canyon Animal Company
Whose dedication to his music
and his animals is astounding as he
continues to create music for animals
www.petcds.com

To
JoJo, the Mighty Yorkie Poo,
Without whose experiences this
amazing tale of life, love and
forever happiness would not be possible
www.jojothedog.com

And to all the other wonderful
no-kill animal shelters and sanctuaries
who give a glimmer of hope to all our
beautiful little creatures .
May God Bless you and all the
magnificent work that you do.

"As JoJo's foster mom who rescued him from Animal Control, I knew he was one special little guy who was very sensitive, smart and required considerable patience and love. Amazingly, JoJo found his perfect 'furever' home with Sande and Mark. Now that he has found true happiness, I think he is on a mission with this book to awaken the world to the fact that all pets and animals truly do have feelings and emotions and need love and security just like you and I. We must all learn to love our little creatures, great and small, and give them the care that they so deserve. In return, we get back much more than we give."

**Sandi Wendt**
**Board of Directors**
**United Yorkie Rescue**

# Mom's Notes

My name is Sande Donahue. I'm JoJo's new Forever Mom. I just needed to take a moment here to tell you a few things about this story and how it all came about.

My husband, Mark, and I adopted JoJo from the United Yorkie Rescue Foundation (UYR), when JoJo was about a year old. One day at work I had nothing to do so I went on the Internet to explore some possibilities of pet adoptions. I had tossed the idea around for a few years and thought this was a good opportunity to see what I could find.

To simply cut to the chase, I found the UYR website and found JoJo's picture. For ten days every day, I went back to that website and to his picture. I was told later that for that ten day period, the foundation received no applications for him although prior to that, they had been coming in on a regular basis. We like to call that Divine Intervention.

When JoJo finally came into our lives, I found his story to be heartbreaking. I knew I had a special connection with our little guy and through his ever-thankful eyes, I always felt that he was trying to tell me something. I contacted Dr. Kim Ogden, a nationally renowned animal communicator and with her fabulous expertise in her field of animal communication, we were able to get information straight from JoJo to fill in the blanks in his story to link it all together. As a result and with the help of many people, I was able to put together an extraordinary story of heartbreak to happiness. And as JoJo would say, his story goes from "horrible to happy."

Since I am a storyteller, I didn't want to present a clinical essay about what we found out. I wanted to weave a tale that would capture the reader's attention and keep them glued to find out what happens to JoJo and his little family. In this process, I used what we like to call our "creative license" and gave you story in which fact and some fiction are intertwined.

I have included in the back of this book a Biblio on Dr. Kim's participation because I want to clarify which points, issues, subjects, comments, etc. came as a result of Dr. Kim's communications. She is not, in any way, responsible for all the content in this book but has been a great help in clearing up certain issues that have plagued JoJo as a result of his experiences. I have written, in detail, those areas that Dr. Kim participated in. To say the least, I was astounded many times with information that she gave us that validated in many ways her abilities as an animal communicator. I will always be grateful to her and will continue to work with her in many areas of animal welfare.

Since JoJo has been with us, it is hard to imagine what our lives were like without him. Loving a pet as much as we love him, changes your life considerably, much like having children. We have adjusted our schedules. We have adjusted our vacation plans. We have even adjusted our list of friends. We discovered that there are folks out there who are not "animal people" and discovered beyond that that these are not folks that we care to be friends with. There is a lack of love somewhere in there and that is distasteful to us. All things being said, this is our "little guy" and nothing, I mean NOTHING, will ever change that forever and a day.

This story is a very hard lesson in loving and caring for pets and animals of all kinds. So if you believe in compassion for our little creatures, animal communication, and believe that animals really do have feelings, emotions, and longings for love, you must read JoJo's story.

I hope you enjoy his antics. I hope you shed a tear or two for the heartbreak of abuse and abandonment. But most importantly, if you believe, spread the word across the globe. That is JoJo's wish for all his pals. He says "it is everything us animals could hope for."

# Chapter 1

"Help! Help! Oh god, somebody help us! Please! We need help!" The words still ring in my ears when I think about those days. There are times when I wake up in the middle of the night, my stomach growling because it's close to morning and almost time for breakfast. But my mind reels back to those horrific days in the basement when my stomach was growling for days, my heart breaking because my mate was almost gone and my child was dazed for lack of food and water.

"Help! Help! My baby needs water! Help!" I knew I had to be the strength and the power if anything was going to happen. If there was any chance at all that we would be saved, it would have to be because I wouldn't give up. When I have those nightmares, my mom jumps awake and quickly grabs me close to her and strokes my head, trying to comfort me. Finally, after a few deep breaths, she snuggles me in her arm and pets me back to sleep as she kisses my head and my ears, reinforcing to me that I'm really home forever and I'm going to be okay.

My name is JoJo. I'm a dog. I have a story to tell that's been locked away inside me for a long time now, a story that desperately needs telling. My hope is that my message and the message of my mate and my child and all those other neglected and abandoned animals will have a voice that might be heard. I'm told that my writing of this book has about as much chance of being heard as a frog in an airline terminal. But I'm willing to take the chance. Who knows. I just might be the loudest frog ever.

It all starts way back when I was just a wee pup. My first recollection is being in a cage with about four or five other pups. Little wee ones just like me. I remember having them and feeling them all around me right from the very beginning, all of us floating together in a warm, soft liquid that was very dark but very comforting. Then one day, we all left the liquid and seemed to just appear in another world. When I first opened my eyes, they were all there and we were all together seeing each other for the first time even though we had already spent many weeks together. Now that I'm older, I can understand that we were all brothers and sisters and we all spent many weeks inside our mother before we came out into the open. Anyway, now that we were out into the world and all in the cages, we slept, we ate, we drank, we peed. That was about it. Every once in a while we'd get this rapturous and joyous energy that would overtake us all. It was almost a memory from somewhere, a very distant place from a long time ago, but can't recall where. We were only four weeks old, so it couldn't have been too long ago. But somehow we knew that we had an instinctive loving energy that came from far away. When we were encased in this rapture, we'd roll around a few times, jump at each other, nibble each other and begin to frolic amongst ourselves. It was a pretty good life considering we didn't know anything else. We were fed on a regular basis, slept when we wanted and played when we wanted. The only problems we really encountered were with five of us in the cage, it could get a little stinky now and then, if you know what I mean. But eventually, our cage was cleaned and we were back to normal.

One day, as we were frolicking and lost in our glorious rapture of fun and frivolity, there were voices from down the way that moved closer to our cage. The voices kept sounding all around us, some low and deep, some medium, some very small and squeaky. Then all of a sudden, one of my brothers was lifted out of the cage. We all ran to the sides of the cage and tried to stick our noses out of the wires to see what was happening. The voices held him for a while as they sounded at one another a few times and then, just walked away. And that was the last time we ever saw him. It was really, really scary. We waited and waited for him to come back, but that never happened. None of us slept that night. We lay next to one another snuggling close, fearful of "what" we didn't know. Was he okay? Was he hurt? Was he hungry? What was happening to him? It was very confusing and frightful and nothing we ever experienced before. Not knowing what had happened to him was overwhelmingly frightful and none of us knew exactly what to make of it. We kept looking down the way to see if he was on his way back, but no such luck. We were very depressed and scared the next day and stayed close to one another. Eventually, as the days passed, we got use to the idea that he wasn't coming back. It wasn't a good feeling, but somehow we knew that we'd just have to get used to it.

      A few days later, our routine got back to normal. But then one day, we heard another set of voices coming toward our cage. We cowered in the back corner of the cage, all together, trembling like we'd never trembled before. The same kind of voices only this time, there was no deep one, just a medium and a little squeaky one. I closed my eyes tight. I was so afraid. And then, like a bolt of lightening, I was lifted out of the cage and up into the arms of one of the voices! I started to scream. "Yip! Yip! Help! Help me! Oh god, help me!" I looked back at the cage and my brothers and sisters were again pushing their noses into the wire. We all started screaming together. Oh god, was it happening all over again? Was I going to be the victim this time? We were in a panic! And then, almost magically, the most beautiful thing happened. I was in the arms of the squeaky little voice and she was holding me like she'd never let me go. She began to kiss me all over and hug me and her little squeaky voice turned into an angelic melody of kindness. I slowly opened my eyes and looked at her. One of the older dogs from another cage hollered out to me. "It's okay, kid! That's a little human girl that wants to take you and give you a Forever Home. Don't be afraid. That's what we all wait for here. Go ahead. Give her some licks to let her know you like her."

I was shocked! A Forever Home? We had heard about those, but were never really sure if they were a real thing. We'd hear the other dogs talk about it like it was some heavenly place. And here I was being picked out to go to one of those places. Was that a good thing or a bad thing? I wasn't really sure, but one thing I do know. The little angelic melody was really getting to me and making me feel warm and fuzzy all over. I blinked my eyes a few times and then, wetting my tongue really good, I gave her a big, big lick on her cheek. Her angelic melody turned into this delightful little shriek! And she kept doing it over and over and the more she did it, the more I licked! I started laughing and laughing and my tale started wagging out of control. I couldn't stop it. I squirmed a little, but not a lot. I didn't want to fall out of her arms or scratch her, but just enough to let her know that I was excited to be with her. All of the other voices sounded back and forth at each other with the little angelic melody shrieking all the time as I kept licking her and licking her and we laughed together like no tomorrow!

All the voices turned. They started walking away from my cage with the little angelic melody following right behind. She still held on to me very tightly. I wasn't frightened any more, but a sadness started to come over me. I looked back. "Hey, bye guys! Bye! I'll be seein' ya'. Take care, will you?" I shouted back to my brothers and sisters in the cage. "Bye, brother! Bye, brother! We love you!" they yipped. "I love you, too!" I shouted back. "Hey, kid! It'll be alright. Good luck to ya'!" Big Dog shouted as I was swooped down the hall and into another big room with lots and lots of windows in front.

The medium voice walked over to a machine with the regular voice that was from our place, the voice that fed us every day and cleaned our cages. The machine opened and the medium voice gave the regular voice a couple of pieces of long green paper. Then I heard the medium voice sound something to my little angelic melody and we walked out a door. As soon as we passed through the door, I was overwhelmed with all the things that paraded before my eyes. I had never, ever seen so many different things in my life. Suddenly, I heard Big Dog in my head telling me some things. We had learned very early on that we were all able to communicate into each other without sounding. Nice trick and quite handy after you learn to master it. But to continue, I could feel that Big Dog was giving me some pretty important information so I paid attention.

"Kid, don't worry. All those things you see are just what exists in the outside world. Those big tall green things that reach to the sky? Those are called trees. Trust me, they can come in very handy. Those noisy machines that you see running around? Those are called automobiles, or cars. That's a human invention. Also quite handy when you need to get somewhere fast. And there are all kinds of humans in all different sizes and colors, but they're still all the same. Just different varieties. But listen, be careful cuz some are good and some are bad. After a while, you'll get to know who's who just by your feel. Hey, have a good life, kid. It can go either way for ya'. So stay on guard."

"Thanks, Big Dog, thanks. I'll do just that."

We kept walking and finally reached one of those noisy machines that Big Dog was telling me about. Medium voice put us in the back and she got in the front. Angelic Melody was still holding me and kissing me. It was a great feeling! I felt like a king! Then all of a sudden, the noisy machine started moving. I watched out the window and everything was zooming past us lickety-split. Wow! I couldn't believe my eyes. What an experience! Wait til the guys back at the cage get a load of this when they get their chance! We kept moving and moving for quite some time. Then finally, we slowed down a little and medium voice stopped the machine. She got out and came around to get us out of the machine from the back. I remembered what Big Dog had said. This was an automobile. This was a . . . car. As we left the back of the car, I looked around and saw the most beautiful place. There was lots of green and tons of those big green things. Trees, I think he said. Whew! They sure were big. As medium voice and angelic melody started walking towards another building, I heard another voice come to me from across the clouds. I have no idea who or what it was. But it told me something very strange, but something that felt so good when I heard it. The voice said that medium voice is to be called "Mom" and angelic melody was to be called "Baby". Okay. That sounded right. It sounded good. No. It sounded better than that. As I bounced those new words around in my head, other words started coming to me. Home. Forever Home. Family. My throat got a little lumpy and a warm tingle wrapped itself around me. I felt this strange tiny little drop of water come out of the corner of one of my eyes. Angelic Melody, I mean "Baby", was still holding me tight. With that, I took a deep breath and closed my eyes. I knew I was in that place that all the dogs had been talking about. I knew I had reached the dream that all dogs dream about. I knew I was in that special place. I knew . . . . . I was in my "forever home".

## Chapter 2

Baby continued to hold me tight as we walked up to a cozy looking building. We passed through a doorway and walked down a long hallway to another door. Mom fiddled around in a pouch-like thing that she was carrying and pulled out a small shiny object that she stuck into a hole in the door. She gave it a quick turn and all of a sudden this next door opened wide. As we walked in, I could smell wonderful scents coming from within and I was suddenly warm. The warmth was a wonderful feeling after being out in the cold.

Baby was still holding me as she walked over to a bunch of fluffy square things that were on the floor. We sat down and she placed me on top of one of these fluffy square things. My, it was soft! I just sunk right into it and lay there, not quite sure what I should do next.

Then, Mom came over and sat down on the floor with us. There we were. The three of us. We were a family. They both had big smiles on their faces and I could feel lots and lots of loving things coming from them as they stroked my head and sounded to one another. And that was going to be a big problem, I could tell. Although they were sounding, I just couldn't understand what it was they were communicating.

And then I heard him. It was Big Dog in my head again talking to me.

"Hey, kid, I can hear ya' all the way over here! You're really having some trouble understanding, aren't you?"

I answered him back in my head. "Yeah, I think I am, Big Dog. They keep sounding to one another, but I just can't figure out what it is they're trying to say."

"Well, that 'sounding' as you call it is what is called 'talking' in human. And ya' gotta give it a couple a days. When you're head clicks in, you'll be able to understand what they're saying. But like a said, it's gonna take a few days."

"Are you sure?"

"Am I sure? Yeah, kid, I'm sure. Trust me. I been around a little longer than you. I know the humans by now and getting used to them is no picnic. But, hey, it's gonna be worth it! I think you're gonna love it!"

"Really? Really, Big Dog? I sure hope so. This is a pretty scary thing here that's going on and getting used to it is not going to be easy for me. Already I miss the gang."

"Hey, kid, when you start to get in the groove, you are going to be shocked. When you're in your Forever Home, you get three squares a day, a warm place to sleep, lots of outside walks, games, you name it. It's somethin', believe me."

"Big Dog, if it's so cool, how come you're sitting in there in a cage? You know so much about it, you must have had a Forever Home somewhere. And how forever can it be if you're there?"

"Well, kid, sometimes life just throws you a curve, you know? My human got sick, went to a big building to get better and never came back. I hear he died. You know, the Rainbow Bridge thing? As a result, I had to go somewhere. But I'm here hoping to get another Forever Home. If not, they're gonna zip me."

"Whadda ya' mean 'zip' you? What's that?"

"Well, it ain't pretty, but it goes like this. When you come to a place like this, you get only so much time to get another Forever Home. And if no one wants you, they have to put you somewhere. And that somewhere is over the Rainbow Bridge. You know, permanent-like sleep. It's where you go to meet up with Sky Dog and he takes you over the Rainbow Bridge and you go to that big meadow in the sky."

"Oh, Big Dog, no! Oh, please don't tell me that. You're gonna find a new human. They're gonna love you!"

"Well, let's hope so, kid. In the meantime, I'm here if you need me. And take it slow and easy. Your new humans look like real nice ladies and they're gonna take good care of you."

"Thanks, Big Dog. Thanks for all the help. I'll talk to you soon, I know."

"You're welcome, kid. Take care now. Bye."

"Bye, Big Dog."

I took another deep breath and mulled over what he had told me. My goodness, what a shocker. I was really scared for Big Dog and hoped upon hope that a new human would come to him real soon. In the meantime, I knew I had my own period of adjustment that I had to deal with. I sat on my big fluffy square thing and just looked around. Mom and Baby were still sounding and then something amazing happened. As they were sounding, I heard *walk* and *outside*. Then I heard *in the morning*. Suddenly, their sounding was beginning to make sense. I was actually understanding bits and pieces, just like Big Dog said. At first, I could only catch a few words and a few phrases. But as I sat quietly, more and more was coming across. Oh my goodness, this was just too much! I was really beginning to love this.

Oh my. Forever Home. Outside walks. Games. It was just too much to take in all at once. This Forever Home thing was going to be a great, great experience. Like Heaven. Well, maybe. We don't want to mention Heaven. Cuz that's connected with the Rainbow Bridge thing. The 'zip' process and all. Oh well, just be glad I'm here. I put my head down on the big fluffy square thing and listened for the rest of the night as my humans, my Mom and Baby, kept talking. And the more they talked, the more I understood. Yeah! I really understood. How cool was that? And how cool was I? Good grief, I was very cool.

After a few hours, Baby put something around my neck connected to a long string. Then she pulled me out the door and down the hall to the outside. We walked across the green stuff under my feet and found one of those big tall green things. A tree?! Yeah, that's what it was, a tree. Whew! And not a minute too soon. I lifted my leg and let nature take its course, if you know what I mean. Boy oh boy, did I need this tree! So that's what Big Dog meant when he said they come in handy. He sure is smart. Yeah, it has really come in handy. And I figured out that we were doing the *outside for a walk* thing.

When I was finished, we went back into the building and there was Mom waiting for us. Baby changed her clothes and put on something called *pajamas* and we went into another room where there was a really, really big square thing. I think they called it a *bed*. Baby jumped on the bed and Mom lifted me onto it with Baby. My goodness, this was a big, big square thing. I mean *bed*. Mom went over to Baby, kissed her nose and then came over by me and kissed my nose. Oooooooo, how nice was that? She picked me up and put me right next to Baby. Baby put her arm around me, Mom walked over to the door, snapped a switch and the room got dark. I closed my eyes and drifted off to sleep. I woke up a few times, but Baby still had her arm around me. What a feeling! Gosh, what a feeling! Zzzzzzzzzzzzz.

*Jojo: A Dog's Tale*

## Chapter 3

I could hear some clanking sounds as my eyes began to slowly open. I still had that adorable arm wrapped around me and was still feeling very warm. Baby had held me tight all night long! I was beginning to feel really, really secure and loved and home. That clanking sound was beginning to get on my nerves but then it stopped. I noticed that Baby had reached over to this little square box on her night table and touched a switch. She rolled over and gave me another smooch on my nose.

I was really beginning to like those kissy things. Makes you feel all warm and cuddly inside. I started to kiss and lick her back and she started her cute little giggles again. I could tell that we were going to get along just fine and be the best of friends.

Suddenly, the door opened and in came Mom with a big tray. She had some bowls on the tray and lo and behold, one of them was for me. I heard Mom and Baby starting to sound and amazingly, I understood every word.

"Happy Birthday, Sweetheart! Our birthday girl deserves breakfast in bed and, of course, our little birthday present needs to have his breakfast, too!"

"Oh, Mom, I love you. And I'm so hungry and I know JoJo is, too!"

"JoJo? Is that his name? Where did you come up with that one?"

"I don't really know. I was just drifting off to sleep and thinking of names for him. I must have thought of dozens and then finally, JoJo just crept in my head and stayed there. I said it a few times and it sounded really good so I decided that's what his name will be."

"Well, alright then. JoJo it is! Here you go, little JoJo. I've got some breakfast for you, too."

JoJo. JoJo. The name kept bouncing around in my head. I really, really liked the sound of it. I was feeling pretty cool by now. JoJo. Yeah, that's me. JoJo.

Baby and I sat quietly next to each other eating and slurping, slurping and eating. This was really the stuff. I'm in a Forever Home with my Forever Humans having breakfast in the big square thing. Or, as they call it, Breakfast in Bed. I was so excited that I forgot that I needed a tree. First mistake.

"Mom! Mom! JoJo just peed in my bed!"

Mom came running into the room with a big cloth, lifted me up and put the cloth under me and ran through the house out the back door. She put me down in the green stuff, the grass, and let me do my thing. I was so embarrassed. I finished my business and just sat there with my head down and my ears flopping. Oh god, what do I do now? Are they going to send me back? Do they hate me? Oh jeez, Big Dog, where are you when I need you?

"Right here, kid. What's up?"

"Oh, Big Dog, I really screwed things up. I got so excited in bed this morning I peed on Baby's bed and now I know they're mad at me."

"Kid, don't worry. Accidents happen and they know that. That's how humans are. They're real good about understanding certain things. They'll get you on a routine where you'll know when you're going to go out and you just learn to control it. Or better yet, if you can't control it, just let them know and they'll get you out of the house."

"How do I do that?"

"Uh, it's called barking."

"Oh. That easy, huh?"

"Yup, that easy. Give 'em a little yip while standing by the door and they get the hint real quick. They're pretty smart cookies, those humans."

"Thanks again, Big Dog. By the way, any luck yet on a new human for you?"

"Nah, nothin' yet. But I keep hopin'. I guess that's all I can do."

"Well, I'll be thinking of you. And I'll keep asking Sky Dog to help you out."

"Thanks, kid. Talk to ya' soon."

"Bye."

"Bye."

Oh boy, I'm really lucky to have someone like Big Dog to help me during my rough times. This human and Forever Home business can be really tricky. I'm going to work really hard to get it all in my head because, for sure, I don't ever want to leave. Oh god, and go back? Never. I wonder how my brothers and sisters are doing. Hey, if I can talk to Big Dog in my head, I wonder if I can talk to my brothers and sisters in my head. Let's see. How do I do this? Think. Think. Think. Hello? Anybody there?

"Hi, JoJo! Hey, JoJo, what's up?"

"Who's this?"

"It's me, MiMi, your sister!"

"And me, Whiskers, your brother!"

"MiMi? Whiskers? Is that what they're calling you? Did you get new humans, too?"

"Yeah, we sure did. And they took two of us and have called us MiMi and Whiskers. We're doing really good, JoJo. How about you?"

"Gosh, I'm doing great. How did you know my name?"

"Oh, we tuned in a little earlier trying to find you and heard the name thing happening. How do you like it?"

"My name? Actually, I love it. Feels really good. Feels me."

"Yeah, it suits you."

"I think it really does suit me. I'm feelin' pretty spiffy, if you must know. How are the others doing? Any word?"

"Oh, they're fine. They've all got new humans, too, and everybody seems to be settled."

"How do you guys like your new humans and your new home?"

"Well, actually, it's pretty hectic around here. We've got a couple of little humans running around all the time and playtime seems to be all day long. By the end of the day, we're pretty worn out. But that's a good thing. Then we have a big meal and then off to bed. And we each have our own bed right in the same room with the little humans. How about you?"

"Oh, I have my own bed, too. It's really, really big and I share it with my little human. Pretty comfy and soft. But I've only got one little human who takes care of me. Baby. And, of course, our Forever Mom."

"Well, good for you. And good for us, too! We're really gettin' into this Forever Home stuff. We really, really love it! I think we're all gonna be fine. Don't you?"

"Oh, we're all going to be great from here on in. I'm so glad you guys found your new humans so soon."

"Yeah, us, too. Hey, JoJo, you take care and we still love you."

"Love you, too, guys. I'll be here whenever you need to talk to someone."

"Yeah, us, too. See ya' later."

"See ya'."

Gosh, that was great! I sure do like this head-talking stuff. Sure saves a lot of footsteps!

Oh, oh, here comes Mom. I wonder if she's still mad at me. Oh dear.

"Hi little JoJo, are you feeling better? You looked so scared when we took you outside. It's okay little guy.

Accidents happen. We'll get you on a schedule and you'll be fine."

Oh, I was so relieved. She picked me up and started hugging me and kissing me and cuddling me all over. I licked her all over her face to let her know that I was okay and also, my goodness, to let her know how much I appreciated her understanding my "accident." I'm going to really try to do better. I sure don't want to make them mad, or worse, want them to get rid of me. I'm really starting to love these two humans. And this cuddling thing is a really good out-of-control thing.

\* \* \* \* \* \* \* \* \* \*

*Thoughts from me to you*

You know, I just have to take a second here and explain how much us dogs really love being petted and talked to and held. If you only knew how much it means to us. And to have someone understand you when you have problems or when you're feeling bad, boy, that's the best. My new Mom is going to be the greatest, I can tell.

We have an advantage because we can head-talk to each other. But we can't head-talk to our humans. Isn't that strange? Yet, we can understand their sounding. The real scary part is that we cannot control our own world. We cannot decide where we're going or what we'll be doing. We have to rely on you humans to take care of everything for us. We are so dependent on you for all our needs and when you take really good care of us, gosh! It's like being in Heaven.

But I know there are a lot of dogs out there that are not only not being taken care of, but they are being neglected and abused. In my travels going through rescue and foster homes, I've run across some pretty disheartening stories, let me tell you. My situation was bad, but some other dogs are really getting a raw deal.

I've heard about puppy mills and dog fighting and just plain abuse by humans. It is so scary to me that sometimes I have nightmares and I whine in my sleep. But much later we'll talk about that. I just needed to take this moment to tell you about kissing and hugging and cuddling and petting and all those good things that you do so well. Please continue for me and all my friends. It's the best!

But, getting back to where we were.

* * * * * * *

Breakfast over and the *outside* thing taken care of, we were off to start our day. I was really curious to see what we were going to do and where we were going to go and just, in general, how things were going to pan out. Well, let me tell you! I was not prepared for this action-packed, new experience-filled whopper of a day.

Where shall I begin?

*JoJo: A Dog's Tale*

## Chapter 4

The sun was shining so brightly it almost made my eyes hurt. The sky was crispy blue with big white puffy clouds drifting across it like they were in a hurry to get someplace. It was already an amazing day and smelling the fresh, new clean air was a delightful experience to behold especially after being cooped up in those cages at the pet store. The humans at the pet store tried their best to keep everything clean, but with so many of us scattered about, it could get a little spicy, to say the least. But this air . . . ahhhhh . . . it was the best!

Baby had me hooked up to the long string (leash, I think they called it) and we scampered through the yard and out the gate to the front of the house. Standing there, to my surprise, were a lot of little humans, all smiling and giggling and grabbing for me. I was a little scared at first, but then I realized that they just wanted to pet me and hold me and, best of all, play with me! Wow! What a day this was going to be!

We all went back through the gate into the fenced yard in the back. It was a big yard and there was no escaping it. The grass was bright green and grassy smelling! There were toys and balls and all kinds of play things. And then, the most wonderful thing happened. Baby took the leash off me and started running around the yard. Then all the little humans began running around the yard, each one calling my name over and over.

"JoJo, come over here!"

"No, JoJo, come by us!"

"Here, JoJo, come get the ball!"

Oh my goodness, this was going to be tricky. How do I play with all of them at the same time? I could tell this was going to really take its toll on me, but hey, I went for it.

I began to run and scamper and jump all over the place. The more I scampered, the more they giggled. One of them threw a little ball over there and I chased after it and grabbed it up in my mouth. Another little human had a tiny rubber doll that she threw in the other direction. I dropped the ball and ran after that little rubber doll. I grabbed it up, shook it like crazy, and all the little humans laughed so hard some of them fell down in the grass. I started laughing myself. I was having such a great time I almost peed again! Hahahaha, what a day this is going to be! Yup, I'm in heaven alright.

We all played for about an hour and then the little humans went over to this box on the ground filled with a very fine dirt-like stuff. They crawled in and sat right in it and picked up some little shovels and pails and began making little houses or castles. I was really glad for the break in play. I was exhausted! While they played, I just lay in the cool grass and rested. I watched them playing their games and doing whatever it was they do in there, but then I just kind of drifted off to sleep. A tiny nap, if you will. They were playing pretty quietly so it was easy for me to catch a wink here or there.

Then, about two hours later, Mom came out the door with a tray of food for the little humans and big pitcher of some colored water.

"Come on, guys, it's lunchtime! I've got some baloney sandwiches and some Kool-Aid here for you so come on over and take a break!"

What on earth is baloney and more importantly, what is this stuff called Kool-Aid? It all actually looked pretty tasty and I wondered if I was going to get any of it. They started eating away and chattering as I just sat there with my eyes all aglow, giving the best "aglow" I could muster. Unfortunately, they weren't impressed as I got none of the aforesaid "baloney." But then, Mom came out with a little bowl and put it in front of me. I put my nose to it and took a big smell. Wowee! This was good stuff. Not like what I had for breakfast, but really good stuff. So, needless to say, I slurped again.

All tasties eaten and done, we started playing again. Then, Baby put my leash back on and we all went out the front gate. All the little humans started running and I, of course, being on the leash, was expected to run right along. I started moving my very tiny legs and running with them. Well, let me tell you. We scampered hard and fast all of us running down the sidewalk lickety-split, laughing and giggling like no tomorrow. I really don't know how long we kept this up, but for sure, I was getting really tired. We all gasped for air and still laughing, stopped for a few minutes to catch our breath. The little humans plopped down on some grass and everybody, once again, was grabbing at me. They all wanted me to sit in their lap and this little rest turned into a real love-fest. Hugging, kissing, petting, cuddling. This Forever Home business is really something. I wish all my friends could have this and then the whole world of us would be happy once and for all. Some day. Maybe.

After collecting ourselves, we got up and began to saunter home. What a great day! We played a little more in the back yard and then Mom came out again. The day was beginning to get really warm, so she pulled out the huge round rubber thing and put it on the ground. The little humans all cheered and laughed and jumped up and down. What on earth was going on?

Just them, Mom went over to the side of the house and came back pulling a very, very long rubber string. Looked like a leash, but yet, it wasn't a leash. It was too long and too thick. I just sat and watched the whole display unfold in front of me. She put the end of the rubber string into the big round rubber thing and walked over to the side of the house again and turned a knob. Just then, a big splash came out of the rubber string and water began to fill up the big round rubber thing. I listened very carefully to try and hear what was going on.

"Mom, oh Mom, thanks for bringing out the swimming pool! It's so hot and this will be perfect."

"Well, you're welcome, honey. Now you kids watch the water and when it gets close to the top, turn off the nozzle and put the hose back by the side of the house."

"Okay, Mom, and thanks."

"And play nice. No rough stuff. You hear me?"

"Yes, Mom."

So this was the new game. It was a swimming pool. Not that I knew what that was or even know what "swimming" is, but I waited along with all the others. Finally, when the "swimming pool" was filled with water, Baby did just what Mom told her to do. She turned off the water and put the hose back by the side of the house. Since it was so hot, all the little humans weren't wearing much clothing so they all jumped into the pool together and began splashing around and laughing again. I watched. I wasn't really sure about this big round rubber thing. This thing called a "swimming pool." Just then, it happened. My worst expectation. They began calling me to come in with them. Oh geez, what do I do now? I sat still, but trust me, somehow I knew this wasn't going to be for long.

Suddenly, Baby jumped out of the water and ran over by me and picked me up and ran right back to the pool. In she jumped with me in her arms and we made the biggest splash ever. Brrrrrrr! Now it was cold compared to the air. The little humans began splashing again and I was getting water in my hair, my eyes, my mouth, my nose. Enough already! I tried to break loose and get out of there, but she was holding me too tightly. Good grief, how am I going to get out of here.

Just then, Mom came out with a bunch of towels and saw me in the pool, drenched and soaking from the dunking. I began to shiver from the cold water.

"What are you doing to little JoJo? Look at him! He's freezing! Don't you know that little creatures like this can't stand as much cold as you can? Here, give him to me."

Mom grabbed hold of me and wrapped me in a big, dry, warm towel. She began rubbing me so I could dry off. Much better. It was then that I realized that I surely was not a "water dog." A little float here and there was just fine with me but I absolutely was not going to be a "swimmer" or a "water fetcher" or any such thing. My preference, actually, was lounging in bed with Baby or on the big floor pillows in the living room or hanging out in someone's arms. Call me fussy, but hey, there are some things that you're just not cut out for and wild swimming and splashing and water logging was not my thing.

So once we got past that little trauma and Baby was able to understand that I was not to go in the pool with her any more, we got along fine. Most of our days were much the same with the occasional ride in the car or walking with Mom and Baby around the neighborhood. I got to meet a lot of other dogs in the neighborhood and each and every one of them said they were having the time of their lives. Each Forever Home was better than the next. Yes, this was surely Heaven that we reached. We were incredibly lucky, all of us. Our hopes were that all of our brothers and sisters could live like us. Some day. Maybe.

## Chapter 5

Life with Mom and Baby was definitely becoming a dream come true. Most of our days were spent enjoying our surroundings and each other, creating a new game here and there and just, in general, living the good life. Little did we know what changes lay before all of us.

I overheard a conversation that Mom and Baby were having and they were talking about some things and new humans that I was unaware of.

"Honey, you better get ready soon. Dad is going to be here in a few minutes to get you."

"I'm almost ready, Mom. Am I going for just a day or for the whole week-end?"

"Well, last I heard, you were going for the whole week-end. Dad is taking you shopping for you birthday."

"My birthday was two weeks ago."

"Yes, but Dad was out of the country on business and couldn't be here. So now that he's back, he wants to take you shopping for some new clothes. Won't that be nice?"

"You bet! You know how I love new clothes!"

"Now I'm going to trust you to buy some nice, decent little outfits for a little girl your age. Don't come home with those little koochie outfits that they're trying put on little kids. I'll make you take them right back."

"Yes, Mom, I know."

"Okay. And I think Dad is taking you out to dinner with his girlfriend, so you be nice."

"Why do I have to go with her. Why does she have to be around? It's MY birthday."

"Just be nice. She's a nice lady and you need to understand that Dad and I aren't together any more and you have to accept whoever he chooses to bring into his life."

"Yeah, yeah, yeah."

Just then, the doorbell rang. Mom went over to answer the door and there stood a man. A rather handsome man with a big smile on his face.

"Hi, John. How are you?"

"I'm fine. And you?"

"Oh, not bad. Come on in. I'll call Lynnie. I think she's ready."

"Lynnie! Your Dad's here! Come on down."

Baby came bouncing down the stairs with a bag of clothes.

"Hi Dad! I want to show you something. Come here."

With that, she took his hand and walked over to me. They both just stood there and stared.

"This is JoJo. This is my birthday present from Mom."

"Well, for heaven's sake. Hey, there little fella. How are you?"

He picked me up and whew, he was big and tall! I was never up this high before. I sure hope he knows what he's doing.

"Boy, you're a cutie, aren't you? What kind is he?"

Mom started to give him all the statistics about me.

"He's a Yorkie Poo. Combination of Yorkshire Terrier and Miniature Poodle. He's about six months old now and quite the package. He and Lynnie are best pals!"

"Dad, can we take him with us? Huh, please?"

Mom answered quickly and was I glad. I wasn't prepared to leave home and try any new adventures with a new human in a new place. I was just getting used to where I was and sure didn't need anything new pushed on me.

"No, honey, JoJo has to stay here. If you and Dad are going to be out running around all the time, who's going to take care of poor JoJo? Are you just going to leave him sit home alone?"

"And besides, where I live, there are no pets allowed. It's a high rise building and there's no place for him to play or go to the bathroom."

"Oh, geez, I'm going to miss him so much!"

"And I know he's going to miss you, too, sweetheart. But the good news is he'll be here when you get back! How's that?"

"Yeah, I know, but I'm still going to miss him."

They gathered up her stuff and out the door they went. I thought about the whole week-end of just me and Mom and thought this would be good. We can both rest and just hang out and be with each other. I knew I'd miss Baby but I also knew she'd be home soon and everything would be okay. A few hours went by. Mom in the kitchen just doing what Moms do and me just hanging around watching her do what Moms do. Then suddenly, the doorbell rang again.

"Now who can that be I wonder?"

Mom went over to the door and opened it. And there stood another man. Another man I had never seen before.

"Brad. What are you doing here?"

"Mona, I had to see you."

"You had to see me? Why did you have to see me? All of a sudden you have to see me. You were the one who made the choices and your choice was to walk out on me and Lynnie, my daughter, who grew to love you like her own father. What do you have to see me about?"

"Mona, can I come in? I want to talk to you. Please, can I come in."

Mom hesitated for a very long time and then she just stepped aside and let this man come into the house. She closed the door and followed him into the living room. They both sat down and began to talk. I quietly crept into the kitchen as I wasn't sure what was going on, but I knew that it didn't involve me, so I scrammed.

About two hours later, Mom came into the kitchen and got two glasses and bottle out of the refrigerator and returned to the living room. It was apparent that this man wasn't going to go anywhere for a while and they just continued to talk and talk and talk. I snuck into the dining room area where I could kind of see them and what I saw was really something! They had their arms around each other and their lips pressed up against each other and they stayed like that it seemed forever!

Finally, Mom broke from the embrace and smoothed her hair.

"You know what? I've got to take JoJo out for a quick walk. I'm sure he needs it by now."

"JoJo? Who's JoJo?"

"He's the little dog I got for Lynnie for her birthday. He's so cute. You're going to love him."

She started calling me.

"JoJo! JoJo, where are you? Come here, sweetie, momma's going to take you outside."

I slowly made my way over to her and the man and just stood in front of them. I figured the best thing to do would be to wag my tale rather quickly. That always gets them.

"Oh, my goodness, isn't he just the cutest thing you've ever seen. Come here, fella."

I walked over to the man, tail still flying in the breeze back and forth, back and forth, and he leaned over to pick me up. Another big and tall strong fellow. Boy, these men sure are big ones!

He held me tight and kept saying how cute I was and what a good boy I was and the usual stuff. They put my leash on and we walked out the door together. Me, Mom and Man. All walking together down the street. It was a rather nice stroll, all of us at a leisurely pace. Then we returned home and I was getting ready to settle in with Mom for a good night's sleep. Suddenly, Mom and Man took each other's hands and carefully walked the stairs up to Mom's room. They closed the door behind them. So much for my night alone with Mom. I just quietly stepped down the hall into Baby's room and jumped up on Baby's bed. It was comfy, but it was sure lonely.

I thought about how lucky I was. But then I thought, if I'm so lucky, why am I so sad right now? I thought of Big Dog.

"Big Dog, are you there?"

"Yeah, kid, I'm here. Whadda ya' need?"

"Oh, Big Dog. I'm sad. Why am I sad?"

"You're sad cuz you've fallen in love with your humans and you're very attached to them. Tonight, your Mom is off doing something without you and your Baby is also off doing something without you. It's just part of life, kid. Sometimes you just have to make do. Everything will be fine. You're just missing your humans. Take it easy and just go to sleep. You'll see. It'll all be fine."

"Okay. If you say so. Thanks, as always, Big Dog."

"Don't mention it. Talk to ya' in the morning. You'll see. You'll feel better. 'Night."

"'Night, Big Dog."

I closed my eyes and let myself drift off to sleep. Alone.

## Chapter 6

The next morning was another bright and shiny day. Mom was already up when I made my way down the stairs. I must have slept in rather late. But then, I'm usually in bed with Baby pretty early and then we get up early. But today, obviously, was a different day. I stayed up late, so I slept late. What a life!

Big Dog was right. I wasn't sad any more. I guess because it was the first time it happened to me, I just didn't quite no how to deal with it. But today, with a new sun and a new day, things were totally fine. I was happy again and we were all together again except for Baby who was still "shopping."

Mom was in the kitchen cooking up breakfast for her and Man. I appeared at the doorway, again wagging my tail.

"There's the little fella! Did you have a good sleep, you little lazy bones?"

It was Man picking me up this time and giving me my morning kisses and hugs. Not bad, this Man guy. He seems to be okay.

"Brad, do you want to take him out back? He usually needs to go out first thing in the morning."

"Sure, I'd love to."

With that, Man picked me up and out the back door we went. He put me in the yard and I walked around, found my spot, did my thing, and was ready for breakfast. We went back into the house and began to enjoy the day. But then, something strange happened. It all started with Mom.

"JoJo, do you like your new daddy? Huh? Yeah, this is Dad. He's going to be living with us."

"So does that mean what I think it means?"

"Yes, it means what you think it means. I do trust you, Brad. But you're going to have to do some real proving to me that you can do it this time. I do love you and haven't stopped loving you. I just know that you are a little boy trapped in a man's body and you've got to grow up and be sincere about taking on responsibilities. You ran out on us the last time because you said 'you couldn't take the pressure.' Pressure of what? Being an adult and holding a job and taking care of a family? Welcome to Planet Earth."

"I know. I know. Two weeks after I left I was kicking myself, but I was too embarrassed to come back and beg forgiveness. Well, things are different now. With this new job and the money I'm making, things will definitely be different. And . . . I've got a surprise for you. Later in the day I'll show it to you."

Okay, I'm thinking to myself what does all this mean? Dad? Living with us? Family? Ultimate confusion. I have no idea what's going on and worse, I have no control over it.

\* \* \* \* \* \* \* \*

*Thoughts from me to you*

Taking another moment here to have a personal thought with you, my reader. Here is a perfect example of what I was talking about earlier. No control. I could not make my own decision as to whether or not I wanted to participate in what the future was spelling out for us. More importantly, even if I could decide, where would I go. I was totally dependent on Mom and Baby, and now, this new *Dad*, and all I could do was go along with the program. It wasn't making me insecure just yet. But it sure was making me wary. When the status quo begins to waver, it's always time to pay attention. Us animals, we don't take to change very well. We can adapt, given time, but change is not a good thing for us. As you will see further down in my story.

\* \* \* \* \* \* \* \*

After breakfast, everyone just kind of lounged around for a while. Mom watched some TV, my new Dad was reading newspapers and I, well, I just hung. Even though I had just woken up an hour or so earlier, my eyes were doing a blink-blink again. But that's just what we're all about. We *love* to sleep and nap and lounge. Playing is good and walking is great, but lounging, that's our thing.

I guess it was about lunchtime and Dad said (*Dad*, this was sounding okay) that we should go out for lunch and then he wanted to show Mom his surprise. So they got dressed and started to gather all the stuff that humans gather to go out with and then, they scooped me up.

"I'm taking you to an outdoor café for lunch and our little guy is coming with us. If he's to be a part of the family, he's not ever going to be left behind if we can help it."

Wow! This Dad guy was really something! I'm likin' what I'm hearin'! Maybe I shouldn't be so wary. Maybe things are going to be fine. I never had a Mom before much less a Dad to go with her. Wowee Wow! A whole and complete family. I've got to really thank Sky Dog for this one! Speaking of Sky Dog, I hadn't been saying my wishes to Sky Dog for Big Dog finding new humans. I will do that tonight just before I go to sleep. I should get in the habit of doing that every night when Baby says her prayers to God. I can say my wishes to Sky Dog at the same time. Perfect. Why didn't I think of that before?

So, off we went into the day headed towards the outdoor café. They sat down under a big, round canvas thing that sort of hung over a table. What was it? Umbrella. Yeah, that's it. Umbrella. Anyway, they ordered some food and I heard Dad order a special hamburger for me. Ohhhhh, I could barely contain myself! A fresh, cooked burger just for me. Food came, they put my burger on a little plate all cut up and let me just nosh away to beat the band. It was so huge, my belly started to round out! But I kept eating. And my belly kept rounding. And I kept eating. What a day! What a Dad! Yeah. What a Dad!

Lunch all finished, everybody gathered up their "stuff" again and we headed back to the car. Naturally, I sat in back hooked up in my special seat. It seemed like we had been driving a while when suddenly the car began to slow down. We were taking some winding roads with lots and lots of trees and some of the biggest houses I'd ever seen! Whew, these were some big houses!

The car stopped and we made a turn into a smaller road that led directly up to a pretty big house. Dad was the first one to speak.

"Well, here we are."

Mom just sat in complete silence looking out the window at this house.

"What's the matter? Cat got your tongue?"

"Brad, I'm not sure what it is you're showing me here or what you're trying to tell me."

"Honey, this is my surprise for you. I was hoping upon hope that you would say exactly what you said today. I've been praying like mad and just to seal the deal and make sure that all my energy was going in a positive direction, I've rented this house for us. With an option to buy, of course."

"Okay, I think I need a little more explanation than that."

"Honey, I love you so much that I am willing to do whatever is necessary to not only get us back together, but with a fresh start and to me, that means new surroundings. You can sell your house, bank the money, and we can all live here. Look at it! It's beautiful! It's big. It's got lots of land for JoJo, it's furnished and the best surprise of all, out back it's got a swimming pool!"

"Oh Brad, it absolutely is beautiful! And a swimming pool for Lynnie and JoJo. But can we afford it?"

"Absolutely! With my new job and new salary, we'll be fine. The rent is a little heavy, but I figure in six months, we'll be settled and we can start working on our buy option negotiations. Come on, babe, whatta ya' say?"

Mom just sat still and then I noticed a little tear running down her cheek. I waited to hear what she was going to say. Truth be told, I wasn't feeling real good about this proposed move. Call it intuition or whatever, but somehow, things just didn't feel right. I liked our other little house. It was cozy and just the right size for me, Mom and Baby. Dad was okay. In fact, Dad was great. But there was something else that just wasn't settling right with me.

"Oh Brad, I love you so. Okay, let's do it. And I'm relying on everything you've said to me. That you've changed and that you are totally committed to us as a family."

"Oh honey, you bet! I am with you 100 percent. A thousand percent! Just give me the chance."

They looked at one another and then they hugged and kissed like no tomorrow! Well, that was really beautiful but, ahem! Helloooo! I'm here!

They both turned around and looked at me. "Well, JoJo, welcome to your new home!"

I have to admit. It was a pretty spectacular place. If everything went according to plan, we were going to be living like Kings and Queens. I was kind of warming up to the idea, but still, in the back of my head, there was this ticking. Tick. Tick. Tick. What exactly was this message that was trying to find its way into my head? I guess I'd just have to wait and see what fate had planned out for us. The concept was exciting, but it was just as scary.

Dad turned the car around and we headed for home, our old home. Our cozy little home. Once back inside, we nestled in for the rest of the afternoon just lounging. Ah. My favorite activity. Whatever was eating me was just going to have to wait a little while longer. It was now lounge time.

*JoJo: A Dog's Tale*

## Chapter 7

The next several weeks was a flurry of activity around our cozy little house. They had put a sign on the lawn and as a result, more and more people kept coming to the house to walk through and look things over. People, people, and more people. It was a never-ending stream of bodies. When these people would come, Dad would grab me up right away and walk away with me into another room. Were they crazy? I needed to get to these people to let them in on the rules. I have rules, you know, and everyone must know about them and follow them! I tried as hard as I could to break loose and get back into the other rooms for the rule business, but Dad just would not let go. Finally, I just learned to sit tight in his arms, stay quiet and wait out the ordeal.

Then one day, I heard Mom and Dad laughing in the kitchen and hugging each other.

"Can you believe it? We finally sold this place. I was getting kind of nervous, weren't you?"

"Nah, honey, I knew you'd do it. You've made this a regular showplace. I knew someone would come along real soon that would fall in love with it. And today was the day. Congrats, sweetie! Now we can get going and get everything packed and get to our beautiful new house."

Mom had lots and lots of big boxes delivered to the house and they were busy every day taking things down and off shelves, wrapping them in paper and packing everything away in those big boxes. I was having a ball tearing through pieces of paper and running in and out of over-turned boxes. Baby and I just played and laughed and I know Mom was a little frustrated at us at times, but then she'd just laugh and go about her work.

Over the weeks, I began to learn lots and lots of new things. I learned that the man in the blue uniform that carries that big pouch full of white paper was called a mailman and I didn't have to bite him or even scare him because his job was to come every day and leave us some of those pieces of white paper and the occasional package. However, being the instinctively well-trained protective entity that I was, I felt it was my job to at least let him know my rules every day when he did come to the house. As a result, it was necessary for me to bark as authoritatively as I could, but refrain from hurting him as badly as I knew I could.

I also learned that running out the door when someone came to the door was not a good thing. A few times Baby got hysterical when I ran out the door and Mom got mad. Not to mention, a few cars that went flying by when I wasn't looking. So that was a lesson well learned. From that point on, when I felt I needed to relate the rules again to whoever, I just stayed on my side of the door and did what I had to do.

Every day there was something new to learn and I was really getting pretty good. I was a quick learner, as they say, and my portfolio of tricks was getting bigger and bigger.

Our cozy little house was looking pretty empty by now. Most everything was packed and ready to go and we just sort of wandered around amidst the emptiness. We managed to still have fun. I still slept with Baby every night. I still went out a few times a day. We would all play in the back yard. We would all take some fabulous walks in the early evening.

The special times were when we'd walk over to this little building and Dad would get us all this wonderful white, creamy yummy stuff that sat on top of a crunchy cone-like thing. I think they called it ice cream. Mmmmmm, was it the best, or what? Yep, this Forever Home business was pretty good.

I was feeling kind of guilty by this time, because I had spent all of my time playing and thinking and doing stuff that was all about me and Baby and Mom and Dad. I was feeling bad because I hadn't given one thought to Big Dog or my brothers and sisters, and worse, I hadn't even said any prayers to Sky Dog. Even though Baby said hers every night, by the time we got to them, I was always so exhausted from the activity of the day, I would fall asleep before Baby was even through with her prayers.

I made a promise to myself that tonight, I was going to take some very special time and try and get into contact with all of them. After all, they deserved a chance for this wonderful Forever Home business and I wanted to stay in touch with each and every one of them to make sure that happened.

Later that evening, when everyone had had their dinner and it was getting close to bed time, I quietly went up the stairs to Baby's room all by myself. I wanted to have a little quiet time to see if I could find anyone through my head talking.

I jumped up on the bed and laid my head down between my paws and just started to think and reach out for someone. First, I called on Big Dog.

"Big Dog, are you there? I've missed you and I'm really, really sorry that I haven't stayed in touch. How are you? Hellooo, are you there?"

"Hey Kid! How's it goin' ? Long time no talk."

"Hi, Big Dog! Gee, it's great to hear from you again. How are things going? Any news on a new Forever Home for you? How about my brothers and sisters? Are they still there?"

"Oh, kid, your sisters and bros are all gone. They were swooped out of here almost right after you. Every day there was some little human in here to get one of those little pistols and take them home. They're all doing great! You should say hello to them when you have a chance."

"Wow, Big Dog! That's really great to hear. I will get in touch with them. But hey, how about you? What's going on with you?"

"Oh, little guy, I'm not at the pet store any more. They've moved me over to the shelter."

"What? What shelter? Why did they move you?"

"Well, you remember when I told you that big, old guys like us don't get swooped up like you little newbies. We kind of have to just rely on someone, anyone, who might have pity on us and take us home just cuz they feel sorry for us. But when that doesn't happen, we can only stay in the store for so long, and when we don't get someone to take us home, they ship us over to a shelter."

"Then where do you go, Big Dog?"

"We go to that big Pet Store in the Sky, peanut. You remember. The Rainbow Bridge and all that."

"Oh, Big Dog, no! No! It can't be! Someone will find you. Someone will love you and take you home! There's gotta be someone out there for you!"

"Well, I ain't too worried about it, kid. I've lived a pretty decent life when I had a life. It'll be okay. Listen, I'll still be able to talk with you. It'll just be from a different place, that's all."

"What? Are you sure? How do you know that?"

"I know that cuz I had a pal like me when I was your age. He was moved over to the Rainbow Bridge and I still talk to him almost every day."

"You're kidding me. Oh, Big Dog, I feel so sad. Is there anything I can do to help?"

"Yeah, you can tell Sky Dog I'm comin' and to get those big, heavenly bones ready! Hahaha! No, I'll be fine. You just take care of yourself and your new family. Live a good life, Little Guy, and think of me often."

"Oh, Big Dog, I will. I will! I'm going to talk with you every day from now on. I'm so sorry that I lost touch."

"Hey, it's no biggie. I knew you were just enjoying your new digs and that's what you're supposed to do. There's plenty of us out there that never get that chance. Think of all those guys and gals in those puppy mills. They never, EVER see anything but those cages. They never feel love and they never get hugged or kissed. So you just go ahead and enjoy what you've got. You have been very blessed by Sky Dog."

"Geez, thanks, Big Dog. Listen, I'll be in touch. You take care, you hear? And remember, you are my best pal, and I . . I . . I love you."

"I'm diggin' you, too, little one. Ta for now."

"Bye, Big Dog. Bye."

After we signed off, I had a lump in my throat. I just made a big sigh and kept my head between my paws. I felt one of those tears start to form in the corner of my eye. Oh gosh, I was so sad. Just then, Baby came into the bedroom and kneeled down beside her bed to say her prayers. I crossed my paws and said my prayers to Sky Dog.

"Sky Dog, please, *please* do what you can for Big Dog. If you can't get him a Forever Home, at least make his journey across the Rainbow Bridge an easy one. *Please!*"

Then I heard that voice from far away again.

*"Don't worry, JoJo. I have it all under control."*

Gracious, was that really Sky Dog talking to me? This communication thing never ceases to amaze me. Tomorrow I'm going to have to see if I can find my brothers and sisters, but for now, I'm just going to ponder all the information from Big Dog. Then, I felt my eyes getting very weary. Big Dog was still swirling around in my head. Gosh, I loved that big guy. He was always there for me. If I could only be there for him. If only I could.

*JoJo: A Dog's Tale*

## Chapter 8

The next morning I awoke to a houseful of confusion. There was a big, big truck parked in the driveway and with it came about five or six big, burley guys. They were moving in and out of the house and with each trip, they carried out a piece of furniture, one of the big boxes, a mattress or two, and they just kept coming and coming and taking and taking. I was beside myself with anger. Who the heck were these guys anyway? Did they think they could just saunter into our cozy little house and start walking away with everything?

I barked my fool head off every inch of the way. Okay, maybe I couldn't hurt one of these guys, but I sure could scare the blue jeans off of them so I just pulled my best vicious right out the barrel! Unfortunately, not one of them seemed too disturbed by me. Okay, let's try that one more time! *Arf, arf, yip, yip, growl, arf!* Still nothing. Well, then, I decided to move into Plan B. Mmmmm, I had no Plan B. So, it looked like it was going to be me against the truck monsters all the way. Just then, Baby picked me up.

"Hey, little poo-poo, those are just the moving guys. They're here to help us take all our stuff to the new house. You be nice to them, okay? They're here to take care of us."

Well, why didn't somebody say something at the very beginning? I wouldn't have had to upset or worry them with my best vicious. Sheesh, you gotta tell me these things, Baby!

The rest of the day I just kind of plopped myself in a corner so as not to get stepped on by one of the burleys. All day they moved stuff out of the house into this huge truck and packed it tighter than a Kibble Bit.

Later in the afternoon, the house was finally empty and the burleys closed the door on the back of the truck. They climbed in and off they went. All of us just sort of stood there looking around. I guess we were all saying our private good-byes.

"Well, guys, looks like this is it. Baby, get JoJo and his bag and let's get going. We want to be at the new house when the movers get there."

Baby held me tight and just kind of walked in a circle. "Bye house. Bye-bye, it was nice knowin' you. I know you're new owner will take good care of you."

I was a bit puzzled. Never experienced anyone talking to a house, but then, what did I know? I was new to this game of life and my learning curve was at an all time high.

Mom and Dad took each other's hands and walked out the door. Baby and I followed while Dad locked the doors behind us. We climbed into the car and began our journey to our new life.

New Forever Home. New Dad. New house. New trees. New yard. Whew! A lot to take in. But we were all ready. I was ready. Baby was ready. Mom and Dad were ready. Off we went.

When we arrived at the new house, it looked like the truck had just pulled up. But they were doing something strange. None of the furniture was being put inside the new house. They were taking out a few boxes here and there, but left most of the furniture in the truck. This troubled me. What was going on?

It was obvious that the load out was not going to take as long as the load in. After they had removed whatever boxes that Mom and Dad instructed them to place into the house, they closed the back of the truck again and took off. Thank goodness for Baby and her inquisitive mind.

"Mom! Where are they going with the rest of our furniture?"

"Honey, if you look around, you will see that this beautiful house is fully furnished. They're taking the rest of our stuff and putting it into storage until we can figure out what to do with it. We might sell it, we might decide to take back a few items, I don't exactly know at this point. But for now, we'll be fine and our furniture will be fine."

"Oh, I was worried there for a minute. I thought we were never going to see it again."

"No, it will be there whenever we want it."

Questions answered, Baby put me down on the floor and started running around the house like a wild girl. I chased after her as fast as I could. We ran and ran and laughed and laughed. Up the stairs, down the stairs, all around the living room and dining room. Out to the patio, back into the kitchen. I was slipping all over the place. The floors were slick as anything and I couldn't get any traction. The more I slipped, the more everybody laughed. We were a sight, Baby and I. Finally, I had to just stop and sit and gasp for breath. I needed water! Mom must have known as she ran to the sink and filled up a little bowl of water for me. She put it down on the floor and I lapped and lapped and lapped. They still laughed at me! I guess I was being a real piggy, but it sure tasted good!

Baby was all collapsed on the living room carpet and was still laughing. I walked over to her and just plopped myself down next to her. She hugged and kissed me and all was good. Mom and Dad just stood in the kitchen, arms around one another, and watched us. This was a good day. I was hoping that they were all going to be good days from now on. Unbeknownst to me, my hopes and wishes were in the process of being wiped away. With all this great stuff that had come into my life, one would think that the journey of the unknown would be close to an end. Alas, my journey into the unknown was about to begin and more treacherous than I could have ever imagined.

Thank goodness for Big Dog. Thank goodness for Sky Dog. Thanks goodness for hope and strength. Little did I know that I was going to need all of them through my journey to come.

## Chapter 9

It took several weeks for us all to get completely settled into our new house. Boxes needed to be unpacked, dishes needed to be put away, drawers needed to be filled with clothes and other goodies that humans needed every day to fix themselves. Not to mention getting used to the house itself. It seemed each one of us would get lost somewhere in the house on a daily basis and the shouting would begin.

"Hey, Brad, where are you?"

"Over here."

"Over where?"

"Here in the library. Where are you?"

"In a nook or crannie somewhere in the kitchen."

And so on it went day after day. At night, Baby would get kind of scared being in a new house and being so big and all and sometimes we would get up in the middle of the night and trot on over to Mom and Dad's room and crawl into bed with them. I, of course, was not about to stay in a new room in a new house all by myself, so they would lift me up on the big new bed and there would be all of us, sound asleep all together until the next morning. It was actually kind of fun and we all had a great time laughing about it.

Week-ends were spent out on the patio and the yard playing by the pool. They even bought me my own special pool float. Boy, what a life. Dad would cook us all kinds of things on the big burning brick box and Mom would make all kinds of good and creamy stuff. Baby loved the yard as did I. We would gallop and gallop around the flowers and bushes and just have a good old time.

This went on for a few months. It was the warm weather time so we had plenty of time to play outside together. Mom and Dad had to leave every day to go to other places. Later, I learned that there was this thing that humans have to do called "work" or "jobs." It's a place that they go to all day to make something called money. I have never been really clear on the whole concept, but then, I'm a dog. I live in a different world. I guess they have to do what they have to do. I'm just glad that I don't have to get up so early every day and trot off to some other place. Not only am I a lounger, I'm a very, very late sleeper.

Anyway, one day when Mom and Dad were due to come home from their work, Dad was a little late that night. When he finally came home, he walked in holding a very big box and put it on the floor. We were all a bit confused.

"What on earth is in there?" Mom asked, standing with her hands on her hips.

"It's a surprise. Can you guess?"

"Uh, no. Can you just show us?"

With that, Dad began to open the flaps of the box and he reached in very carefully as he kept grinning from ear to ear. Then, like magic, out came this . . . oh my gosh, . . . out came this fabulously stunning female. I mean she was beee-yoooo-tiful! Look at those eyelashes! Look at that silky coat! Look at that body! My heart was beating so fast I thought it might hop right out of my chest and across the floor.

"What on earth do we have here?" Mom reached out to pick up this gorgeous creature.

"One of the guys at work has to get rid of her. He's moving out of state and doesn't really know where he's going to be living and whether or not he can have dogs, so he was looking for someone to take her and give her a good home. She's a pedigreed miniature Pomeranian and her name is Lily. And I thought . . . well, I thought we could certainly give her a good home. We have plenty of room and we love animals and I think JoJo could use a playmate. What do you think, hon?"

"Oh, I think she's adorable. Should we really?"

"Why not? We've got all the components and they all fit together which, to me, makes a perfect fit."

My heart was still beating a hundred miles a minute! Here? Live here? With us? Forever? How did I get so lucky? She was really something. This gorgeous creature just sat in Mom's arms and looked around the place like she already owned it. As far as I was concerned, she did! What a dish! What a gal! What a . . .

"Hello."

*Hello?* HELLO? Was she talking to me?

"I said 'hello.'"

"Uh, uh . . . hello. Yes. I mean . . . hello."

"My name is Lily."

"I'm JoJo. Guess you're going to be living here."

"Yes, I guess I am. What's it like here?"

"Oh, it's great. Just great. Lots of room, good food, good humans. Yeah, it's great. Uh, did your humans leave you?"

"Well, I guess they had to move away and couldn't take me with them. Kind of sad, but they were gone most days and I was left alone. Good home, but kind of lonely."

"Aw, you won't be lonely here. My mom and dad work, but then Mom and Baby get home early in the afternoon. But then, you'll always have me. I .. I mean . . . "

"I know what you mean. And I appreciate that. It'll be nice to have a friend around all day. At least we can play together or talk, or do whatever we want."

"Yeah, yeah, that'll be nice."

Holy moly, I'm gonna have this gorgeous creature around me all day long. I sure hope she doesn't get tired of me. Or get mad at me. Or . . .

"Stop being so paranoid. I can read what you're thinking."

"Oh yeah, we do that, don't we? What's paranoid?"

"It means when you're thinking bad things are going to happen when they really aren't. That's paranoid."

"Oh."

"So you can relax. I can tell we're going to be great friends, JoJo. You just seem like the type that everyone likes."

"Yeah, that's me. Everyone likes me. Well, I mean . . . I hope everyone likes me."

"Again, I know what you mean."

I could tell the conversation between me and Lily was coming to a temporary close. Mom put her down on the floor and she began to prance, yes, I said prance around like a Princess. What else did I expect? She was, of course, a virtual Princess. So beautiful. So elegant. Goodness, how was I going to contain myself around this magnificent being?

As time went by, we all became one big happy family. Lily and I had become very close and I could tell she began to rely on me for a lot. I think she kind of took a shine to me. Of course, the feelings were quite mutual and I did everything I could to make her feel comfortable and safe. Baby loved playing with her, but Lily was certainly a little more delicate when it came to our jaunts around the yard. I was more rough and tumble and she was more . . . well, . . . prancee. Her long, beautiful fur would flow in the day breezes and her sweet little ears would catch in the wind and sometimes make her look like she had angel wings. Hahaha, it was a delight to watch her.

Mom and Dad and Baby had made some rather keen adjustments in the house, too, with regard to Lily. Now, there were two matching bowls for water and two matching bowls for our food. We seemed to have doubled up on some toys and the big thing was the new bed. I no longer slept in the bed with Baby. Mom and Dad had bought a big, beautiful doggie bed that was put on the floor next to Baby's bed. That's where Lily and I started spending our nights. Together.

It was really warm and cozy in that bed with her beside me. Sometimes, in the middle of the night, I could feel her inching a little closer to my side and then she'd take a deep breath and just kind of nuzzle in beside me. I didn't dare move because I didn't want to break the moment. I just pretended to be asleep and let her come and nuzzle. It was grand. And she always smelled so good. I have to say at this point that I was becoming keenly aware that our "friendship" felt like it was developing into something else. I think you get my drift.

She had a way about her that just sort of pulled you in right from the beginning. And . . . made you feel that you were the most important thing around. She made you feel like a great warrior of some kind. She made you want to protect her. She made you want to love her. Yes, I loved her. And you know what, I know she loved me, too. She didn't have to say a thing. It was in her eyes and the way she would nuzzle me at night and the way she would poke her teeny little nose at me during the day. When she flashed those dark eyes and those long lashes at me, I was a goner. And she knew it.

But that was okay. We both knew. And we both liked it. One night, when she slipped over to nuzzle me in bed, I decided that I would let her know that I was awake and aware. I pushed closer to her. She gently licked the side of my face and the tip of my nose. That night, we decided that it was going to be her and me for the world to see. That night, we became one.

# Chapter 10

As the days and weeks went by it was grand and we were all happy. For a while.

One of the days that Mom and Dad didn't have to leave to go to their jobs, Dad got up real early. He was getting dressed when Mom woke up.

"Morning, honey. What time do you tee off?"

"In about half an hour. I'm meeting Kevin and John at the course."

"Okay, well, have a good game. We're just doing burgers on the grill tonight, so nothing special. Just don't be late."

"Gotcha. See you later."

With that, Dad went downstairs and grabbed this big bag full of some metal sticks, put it into the back of his car and left. Didn't seem like anything out of the ordinary. Mom, Baby, Lily and I just hung around the house all day. Mom did some work around the house, Baby played a little, I lounged. Another one of those great lounge days! Ah, life was good.

Mom saw to it that we all had a good breakfast, then later in the day we had lunch. Dinner, of course, was going to be done with all of us including Dad when he got home. Therein is where the problems began.

I know it was nearing dinner time because my stomach was beginning to growl. I knew that Baby was hungry, too, because she was getting cranky. Mom was walking around the house and patio with a glass of wine. She paced and paced. She had prepared all the food for dinner earlier in the day but hadn't put anything out yet. I assumed she was waiting for Dad. Finally, when the sun had begun to sink further down on the horizon, Mom lit the brick burning box and made us all our grilled burgers. She brought out the other food and the three of us just kind of huddled around the table out on the patio.

Not much was said between Mom and Baby. But you could tell that Mom was not in a good mood and Baby didn't want to upset her any more than she had to. Lily and I just ate and disappeared out on the grass. I could sense that things were not well and things were going to get worse.

The sun had finally disappeared completely and Mom put some lights on. Suddenly, we heard the garage door opening. Mom just sat. Then we heard the door open in the kitchen that leads to the garage and heard the garage door closing. A jingle here, a jangle there, keys and coins being placed somewhere on the countertops, and still nothing was said. Finally, Mom spoke first.

"Brad, we're out here."

"Yeah, I figured. Be there in a sec."

"No, now, Brad."

"I said in a second!"

With that, Mom jumped up and raced into the kitchen.

"Where the hell were you? Can't you call? We were all waiting for you for dinner."

"Big deal. Burgers. What's the problem?"

"You're drunk."

"Yeah, I'm drunk."

"Brad, is it starting again?"

"Is what starting? Jesus, woman, cut me some slack. I just got caught up with some of the guys, we drank, we talked, next thing I knew, it was late. We were all there together."

"Brad, this can't start again. I won't have it. This time it's after a Saturday golf game. Then it moves to Wednesday and Friday nights. Then it moves to every night. This can't start again."

"Babe, one night. Geez, I haven't been out with the guys in months. One golf game. One night. Relax, will ya'. Sorry I missed dinner, but trust me. If it were ribs or steak, I'd have made it my business to be here. Hahaha, nothing but the best for this guy!"

He moved toward Mom. She pulled away and came back out to the patio. Lily and I still hung out in the grass. I had no clue what was going on, but the vibes were not good and I didn't want to be anywhere around this interaction. I could tell that Lily was getting very, very nervous.

"JoJo, what's going on in there? Are they going to be okay?"

"I don't know, Lily. I just don't know. I don't know what 'drunk' is, but if it's anything like that smell that's coming from Dad, it isn't good. Just stay out here with me."

Mom and Dad started their conversation again which was quickly escalating to something other than a mere conversation.

"Brad, don't try and be funny with me. You are NOT funny."

"I'm not trying to be funny with you. I AM funny. HA HA! There! Get it?"

"Is that all you're going to say? You know, you really have not changed at all. You just managed to hide yourself for a few months. Just long enough to get us sucked in again and then you just went right back to the old Brad. The old drunken Brad."

"Yeah, the good old drunken Brad. What a guy, huh?"

"Well, I'm not going to try and reason with you in this state. I'm going to bed."

"What's to eat?"

"Nothing is to eat. We ate, cleaned up and that's it. You figure out what you're going to eat."

"Listen, you sad excuse for a woman, fix me something to eat!"

"Brad, I'm warning you. If this keeps going, I'm going to call the police."

"Oh, that's rich. She's going to call the police. Is that all you know how to do?"

"Good night."

With that, Mom just turned around and went for the stairs with Baby following right behind. Lily and I stayed behind in the grass. I wasn't about to cross paths with Dad in that state. Thank goodness it was warm weather time because I had a feeling that we were going to be left out all night. My mistake. Suddenly, I heard Baby crying out as she bounced down the stairs.

"JoJo? Lily? Where are you? Come inside and go to bed. Where are you?"

I jumped up and started barking. I knew if she heard me she would come and get us right away. I was right. She ran to the patio doors and opened them wide for Lily and I to go through. We ran lickety split past Dad up those stairs and right into her bedroom. We both nestled into our beds immediately hoping that Baby would come right behind. She did just that, closed her door tight, and turned off the light. I could still feel the tension in the air, but at least we were safe and inside. Tomorrow would be another day. Tomorrow would turn a new page. Little did we know that it was going to be a series of blank pages. The beginning of our journey into the unknown which can only be best described as . . . hell.

*JoJo: A Dog's Tale*

## Chapter 11

The next morning Mom and Baby were already up and getting breakfast ready. Lily and I, as stressed as we were the night before, must have been exhausted from it because we slept in really late. We both stretched and shook ourselves a little and began to make our way down the stairs.

"There's my two little guys." It was Baby. She seemed no worse for the wear and was just sitting quietly at the table munching on some toast and juice. Mom filled our bowls and set them down in their usual spot. She returned to the kitchen stove and continued cooking up some bacon and eggs, I presume.

"Brad, get up. Breakfast is on the table."

"Mmmmmffffmmmphph. Where's the aspirin?"

"In the medicine cabinet where it always is. Head feeling a little tender today?"

"You betcha. I'll be right down. And don't shout at me when I get there."

A few minutes went by. We could hear Dad rustling around in the bathroom, running water, brushing his teeth, doing those human things, when he finally started down the stairs.

"Mmmmm, smells good. Any coffee brewing?"

"Of course, there's coffee. When did you ever get up in this household without morning coffee? Forgetting where you're at?"

"Okay, don't start. Let's just try and start the day out under some normal vibes, okay?"

"Listen, I wasn't the one who blew dinner with the family and came home snarked to the gills."

"I'm sorry. What else can I say?"

"Nothing, I guess. I'm just going to start keeping score, that's all."

"Whatever. You just go a head and do whatever it is you think you have to do."

Then there was silence. This was the second day of their two-day break from work and we all usually just lounged around the house and yard. My favorite thing to do but today I knew I wasn't going to get any pleasure from it.

My first thought was to Big Dog. I needed to get in touch with him desperately to see if I could get any answers to this perplexing situation that was developing.

"Big Dog? Big Dog, are you there? Big Dog!"

"Yeah, kid, I'm here. Nice to hear from you. What's up on your end. How are you and your honey getting along?"

"We're getting along really fine, Big Dog. In fact, we're in love!"

"Well, hey, I knew that was gonna happen. How long do you think a handsome guy like you can stay alone?"

"Ha ha, very funny, Big Dog. But thanks. Listen, I've got a problem going on here."

"What's the deal? How can I help?"

"Well, I guess you can help me by simply giving me some answers. My humans are NOT getting along and things aren't real happy around here these days?"

"What's up? Why aren't they getting along?"

"It all has to do with this thing that Dad does. He goes out of the house and doesn't come home for many hours and when he does come home, he smells terrible. From his breath."

"Ahhh, I know it well. It's called alcohol. Listen, kid, you be careful, you hear me? That alcohol thing can get real nasty."

"What do you mean?"

"Well, when humans drink this stuff called alcohol, sometimes they can get all screwed up in the head and it messes with their reasoning power."

"Like saying bad things when you really don't mean it?"

"Yeah, exactly like that. And worse, doing things that you don't mean to do and worse even than that is hurting other people or things, like us animals. I've seen some dogs get hurt pretty bad by drunk humans. Just be aware and stay away. Remember, I told you a long time ago that with these humans, some are good, some are bad. You just have to know which is which."

"Thanks, Big Dog. I will be careful. You take care."

"Yeah, you, too, kid. Take care."

Whew! I sure wasn't ready to hear that. Now I was really concerned about our future. And my poor Lily. I was doubly concerned for her. She'd been looking a little under the weather the last couple of days and I sure didn't want her to get sick and then have to deal with what was going on in the house on top of it.

"Well, what did Big Dog have to say?"

"Oh, just that we need to be aware and keep ourselves kind of apart from the activity around here."

"Well, while we're on the subject of keeping ourselves apart, I'm afraid we will have to be doing that no matter what."

"Why, Lily, what do you mean?"

"JoJo, I'm having our puppy."

"What?!"

"I'm having our puppy. A baby. A wee one."

"Oh my gosh, my sweet angel! I am so happy I can't tell you. When? When did you know? When did it . . . never mind, I think I know the answer to that one. How do you feel? Are you okay?"

"I'm fine. I just need to rest and eat good and everything will be okay."

"When are we due?"

"In about 51 darks, at the most."

"51 darks? That soon? Oh my goodness, we better get ready!"

"And do what?"

"Well, actually, I don't know."

"All we have to do is sit tight and just make sure that I get plenty of rest."

"Okay then, if that's what we have to do, then that's what we'll do. Can you still go up the stairs? Can you come down to eat? How does all this work?"

"Honey, I'll be fine. Yes, I can go up and down the stairs and I will be able to come down and eat. What I need to do is rest most of the day. I won't be able to go out and run around with you and Baby every day, but I can sit on the sidelines and watch you play."

"Well, whatever you need. You just let me know, okay?"

"Okay, sweetie, thank you."

Wow! A baby! Gotta tell Big Dog! Gotta tell Big Dog!

"Big Dog, are you there? Are you there? Gotta talk, guy."

"Hey, kid, I'm here. Whadda ya' need?"

"Big Dog, get this? I'm gonna be a father! Can you believe it?"

"No kiddin', kid! Wow! That's really great. Congratulations to you and Lily. Say, what kind are you now? I forget."

"I'm called a Yorkie Poo. Half Yorkshire and half Poodle. It's okay, I guess, but no designer dog here."

"Whadda ya talkin' about? Yeah, you're a designer dog!"

"Shhhh, don't let that get around, okay? Kinda keep it to yourself."

"Well, I got a question. If you're a Yorkie Poo and Lily is a Pomeranian, does that make your kid a Yorkie

PomPoo!? Hahahaha, I think that's great! How do ya' like that one?"

"You are such a goof! But truer words were never spoken. I got to tell that one to Lily. She'll love it."

"Well, congrats, kid. Let me know when the package arrives and I'll let all the old crowd know."

"Will do. How's the shelter? Any bites yet on a Forever Home?"

"Nah, nothin'. And I don't expect anything. They say I've got about 2 or 3 days left."

"No! No, Big Dog, no!"

"Yeah, kid, that's the way it is. Hey, we talked about this before. Settle down. It'll be okay."

"Oh, Big Dog, I can't tell you how I feel. I'm so . . so . . "

"Don't worry about it, kid. I'm gonna sign off fer now. Gotta go eat. Hugs to the little lady, okay?"

"Yeah, thanks, Big Dog, thanks."

I just sat with that lump in my throat again. This roller coaster ride of life was beginning to get to me. Good news. Bad news. Good news. Bad news. Does it ever even out? Does the pain ever go away?

I decided I was going to focus on Lily and the puppy. And I couldn't let her see me like this. *Big Dog, I love you.*

*Love you, too, kid.*

"Lily, it's time to eat. Let's go get some nutrition in you, okay?"

"Okay. Let's"

Tomorrow. Another day. Another page. I wasn't sure I wanted to keep turning the pages. But forge ahead I would. I had my own family to think about now. I had MY Baby to think about.

*JoJo: A Dog's Tale*

## Chapter 12

The next couple of days were relatively quiet but you could tell that there was still tension in the air. Mom and Dad spoke to one another and they, of course, interacted with Baby and the rest of us, but you could tell that their focus was clearly not on what they were doing at any given time.

My Lily was doing well but she mainly stayed upstairs in our bed and only came down to eat or get some water. She was starting to bulge a bit and I was concerned for her. I was just laying on the carpet in the living room when I saw her coming down the stairs. She looked like she was having a bit of trouble and I didn't know for sure if she'd be able to make it back up those stairs. Then I heard Mom.

"Lily, honey, are you okay? You look a little droopy. Are you feeling alright?"

Just then, Mom reached down to pick her up and hold her.

"Oh my god, guess what, folks."

Baby was sitting at the kitchen table.

"What Mom?"

"It seems our little Lily here is with child. Or children, in her case."

*Children?* Did that mean what I thought it meant? It only made sense. I had a couple of brothers and a couple of sisters. That means . . . oh goodness. That means us dogs don't just have a child. We have lots of childs! Or children! We were going to have *children!* As in more than one. We were going to have a litter of puppies! It was all coming clear now. Our natural instincts have a way of surprising us when we least expect it. I hadn't even given it a thought before, but my instincts were now kicking in and the whole picture was coming clear. I could only react with GET READY!

Dad moved into the kitchen and felt Lily's belly.

"Well, I'll be! You little devils you. And you JoJo, you man-about-town. She's not even with us three months and you're already making babies. You go, boyfriend!"

"Oh, take it easy, Brad." Mom started to giggle. "What did you expect? Neither one of them have been fixed. It was bound to happen sooner or later."

"So does that mean we're going to have a houseful of little things running all around? Can we handle it?"

"Oh, I think we can handle it. Listen, there's plenty of girls at work that would just love to have one of their puppies. Everybody thinks that these two are just the berries. They'd take them in a minute."

"Well, this is your little project. I don't want any part of this three-ring circus."

"Oh, don't you worry your pretty, little stupid head about it. We'll take care of everything. Just like we always do."

"What the hell is that suppose to mean?"

"Nothing. Just go back to your newspaper."

I was not feeling good about this exchange of words. This is how it always started. A few words here, a few words there and ka-boom. We're right back at it.

"You know, I'm really getting fed up with your insinuations."

Dad went to the coat closet, took out a jacket and put it on quickly. He grabbed his car keys and moved towards the door.

"Where the hell do you think you're going?"

"I'm going somewhere, anywhere, where I can get some peace. And maybe someone nice to talk to. Someone who won't try and cut me to shreds with every word."

"Don't you dare leave this house!"

"Bye." And out he walked.

Lily and I made our way up the stairs and went to our bed while Mom and Baby went to theirs. A few hours later, Lily woke up and said she needed some water so she and I went down the stairs to the kitchen to get a nibble and have a little drink of water. While we were at the water bowl, we heard the garage door opening. It was Dad returning from his outing.

As usual, after he would do one of his disappearing acts, he returned not in the best of shape. He came through the door, stumbling and mumbling. He had that familiar but distasteful smell all around him and he kept stumbling around the kitchen when he came in from the garage. Mom must have heard him making a racket. She started coming down the stairs tying her bathrobe together. I could see that she was not pleased.

"Where the hell have you been? And look at you, you're drunk as a skunk!"

"Yeah, I'm drunk alright. So what?"

"Brad, this has got to stop or we need to re-evaluate where we are together. I can't go through this all over again."

"Oh, little lady. She can't go through it all over again. Boo hoo. Whatever will she do?"

Lily and I decided it best if we just get out of there and go back upstairs. We headed around the center island and tried to make our way toward the stairs. Just as Lily was mid-way between the island and the stairs, *wham!* He kicked her. *He kicked her!* She went flying across the floor sliding on her side.

"Oh, ouch! Oh, gosh, oh, it hurts!" Lily cried. She just lay limp.

With that, I lost my head.

*"Arrggghh! Grrrrrr! Arf, arf, yip, yip, arrgghh, grrrrrr!"*

I went after him with every thing I could muster up. I was growling, barking, spitting, drooling and going after any piece of flesh I could find on him. Unfortunately, I found none. I couldn't get close enough to him. He kept stepping and prancing and kicking to stay away from me.

He gave one good, powerful kick. Another *wham!* He caught me in my face.

*"Yip, yip, yip, oweeee, yip, yip!"* I screeched. I really tried not to appear to hurt or scared, but truth be told, he really caught me a good one. I stayed near Lily just in case.

Just then, Mom went into action.

"You bastard! Who the hell do you think you are?" She went after him with all her strength. She began whacking him all over. His face, his chest, his shoulders, the back of his head. She didn't care. Amazingly, he didn't raise his hands to her at all. He just put his arms around his head and face to try and protect himself from her wrath.

"Aren't you the big man?" she continued. "Aren't you just the hero? Going after two tiny, little dogs! And one of the pregnant! You big jerk!"

She started whacking him again. If we weren't in such pain, it would have been comical. But, alas, both Lily and I were not in great shape. We carefully picked ourselves up and made our way to the stairs and started our ascent. It was not without great effort, believe me. We slowly made our way to the top and limped our way into Baby's bedroom and into our bed. My poor Lily.

"Lily, are you okay?"

"Oh, I'm surviving, I guess. How are you feeling? Are you okay?"

"Well, I caught a good one in the face. Kind of feels like my bone got cracked or something. But I'll survive, too."

I heard Mom coming up the stairs.

"Just stay down there tonight. I don't want you anywhere near me, you rat! Just stay away from me til I can stand you again. And trust me, there is no guarantee that's going to happen."

I could hear Dad downstairs still attempting to make his way around the house. I could hear him pull out a pillow and blanket from one of the linen closets downstairs and he made his way to the sofa and finally plunked down for the night.

Everything quiet and calmed down, we all settled in for the night. It was difficult trying to get to sleep. I was really worried about my Lily and worried about what the future was going to bring. But the truth of it all, I knew I had no control over anything. I thought about us running away, but where would we go? What would we do? How would we survive? We were not the kind of dogs that could live in the wild or run the streets. We were special dogs with special backgrounds. We were just special. At least my Lily was. My poor Lily. She did nothing to deserve this. Or this kind of life. How was I going to take care of her.? I felt helpless. I was helpless. I was just a dog.

## Chapter 13

Several days past and things were quiet. As usual, there was this tension that hung over all of us like a cloudy day. We all went about our usual daily business, but there was no joy, no playtime, nothing that even resembled happiness or family. I decided to get in touch with Big Dog. He always made me feel better and always had some kind of Big Dog wisdom to throw my way that always gave me a better insight to things.

"Hey, Big Dog, are you there? I need to talk to you."

"Sure, kid, I'm here. What's up?"

"Oh, pretty much the same problems and issues that I told you about before. Nothing has changed in that regard. Lily and I took some blows a while back, but we'll make it through. I'm still a little sore in my face and Lily is still a little sore, but for the most part, we're okay. How about you?"

"Well, funny you should ask. I'm on my way to the "Big Sleep." Heh heh, kinda funny, doncha think? You callin' me right at my special moment?"

"Big Dog! Don't tell me! Please! You mean . . . you mean . . ."

"Yeah, kid, I'm right there. I'm on the table now."

"Oh no! Oh no! Oh, Big Dog..."

My eyes were watering, my throat was dry. My special friend was leaving me and neither one of us had any control over the situation. Oh, Sky Dog, Sky Dog, why are we like this? Why can't we have some kind of control? My eyes were filled with water.

"Hey, kid, don't you worry. I told you that this was really going to be easy. They just stick a needle in you and you go to sleep and on to the Rainbow Bridge. I'll be fine."

"Oh, Big Dog, I wish... I wish..."

"I know, kid, we all wish. But sometimes, those wishes don't come true. Hey, listen, you take care of that little lady of yours. And those kids that are comin'. I'll be thinkin' of all of you all the way. And don't worry, I'll be in touch."

"Big Dog, I know I haven't said this much. But I love you. Do you hear me? I LOVE YOU! You have been my best friend!"

"Kid, I love you, too. Always did. You're a fighter. And you stay that way. You'll do good. Here they come. Oooo, ouch, that was a little sticky with the pin. But it's okay now. You just live a good life and think of... me when... you... can...and..."

"Big Dog?! Big Dog?!" He was gone. He.. was.. gone. My friend. My pal. I hung my head.

Lily licked my face. "What's the matter, hon?"

"It's Big Dog. I was just talking to him and they put him to sleep. Right when I was talking to him. Oh, I could just die."

"Oh, JoJo, I am so sorry. I know how much he meant to you. Is there anything I can do?"

"Yes, just stay near me. You are my only solace right now."

I put my head down and wept. I guess the pain was too much. I drifted off to sleep with my Lily by my side.

I must have slept for an hour or two when I felt Lily nudging me.

"JoJo, something's happening."

"What? What's happening."

"I think it's time."

"Time? Time for what?"

"Time to have babies, you silly goose!"

"Oh! Oh! Okay, oh, oh . . ."

"Calm down. It happens every day. Maybe you should go and get Mom."

"Oh, okay, I'll be right back."

I ran down the stairs as fast as I could barking all the way. I stood on the kitchen floor and looked up at Mom and barked and barked and ran back and forth to the stairs. I was so glad that today was not a work day for Mom and she was home right there with us.

She got it right away and came running right behind me as we both bolted up the stairs. Mom called Baby in from the outside and they both hovered over Lily while she grunted and pushed and squirmed.

"Does it hurt, Lily, does it hurt? Can I help you?"

"No, silly, just stay calm and watch your babies come into the world."

So I obeyed her every word. I just sat still and waited for the miracle to happen.

I could see her stomach contracting in and out, her little legs just laying limp beneath her. Suddenly, we could see something between her legs. Oh, it was wet and mushy looking. Oh, it was not a pretty sight. I was not feeling good in my stomach. Ick.

She pushed and pushed and out it came. Mom was right there to pick up the little being. She held it up and looked at it. She didn't have that joyous look and expectation in her face that I felt she should have after helping to birth and little being.

She looked mad. She looked sad. She spoke to Baby.

"This one didn't make it."

"Mom, what do you mean?"

"I mean this one didn't make it. She's dead."

Lily looked horrified!

"Oh, JoJo," Lily began, "what did I hear her say?"

"Uh, I'm not sure, sweetie."

"Listen to her. Listen carefully. Tell me what's going on."

I watched Mom as she kept looking at our new born. She did not look hopeful.

"Sorry, honey, it looks like little Lily is having a problem. This one didn't make it."

"Oh, Mom, how awful! How did this happen? What are we going to do?"

"We are going to do nothing. We'll just have to bury it out in the backyard. And to how it happened, I don't even want to approach the possibility of how it happened."

"Do you think . . . do you think . . .?"

"I'm afraid so. It was the kick she got."

"Oh, Mom!"

Baby began to cry. I was dumbfounded. I was drained. I was angry! If I could have been a lion or a tiger at this point, I would have eaten that man alive the minute he walked through the door.

Mom kept talking.

"Listen, we've got to keep going here to see what's going on with her. Let's pay attention."

Lily's eyes were filling up with water. I stayed near her and licked her face when I could.

"Here comes another one! Look, Baby, here's number two!"

The second little baby came right out looking just as slimy as the last one. I sure was not cut out for this birthing business!

Mom took the little baby and held it up high just like she did the last one. Again, she did not look good.

"Another bad one."

"What? You mean this one's dead, too? No!"

"I'm afraid so. She's really having a tough time of it. But listen, it's good that they're coming out and not staying inside her. She could get very, very sick if that happened."

I was beside myself! But I had to keep my cool because it looked like Lily was on the edge.

"Mom, look, look, another one!"

Mom reach for a third one. Again, a slimy little creature. But this time, something different was going on. This time there seemed to be a little movement in this tiny creature. It looked like its little legs were moving about.

"This one's good! This one's okay!"

She put the tiny baby down along side Lily as Lily began to lick and lick the slimy covering off of her. I moved in closer to try and help, but frankly, couldn't stand the smell or the looks of the stuff, so I just sat looking my best brave self.

Mom stayed with us for a while to make sure that there were no more babies coming. She felt Lily's stomach a little, moved her fingers around her belly to see if there was anything left inside.

"She seems to be done. Looks like there were only three. Too bad the other two didn't make it."

"Yeah, too bad. Maybe we should keep them and serve them up to you-know-who for dinner."

"Oh, honey, there's nothing we can do about it now. Let's just be thankful that we have at least one healthy one. Don't worry, there are going to be some changes made."

"Again?" Baby asked.

"Yes, again. I'm sorry to put you through all this, but I have to do what's best for the both of us. I thought the move here was going to be good, but we were fooled, weren't we?"

"Yeah, we sure were."

Mom and Baby went downstairs and brought up our food and water bowls. I guess all meals and water were going to be had right here in the bedroom for a while to come. That was okay with me. The less I had to go down stairs and mingle the better I liked it.

I looked at poor Lily. I could tell she was a bagful of emotions. She was thrilled at her new baby, but was still reeling from the loss of the other two. I stayed close to her for the next couple of days and did what I could to make her comfortable.

My emotions weren't exactly in tip-top shape either. The loss of Big Dog was still lingering in my head and now to compound it, I lost two of my very own children. What else does life have to throw at me? Big Dog said I was a warrior. Well, I've got news for you. Even warriors cry.

*JoJo: A Dog's Tale*

## Chapter 14

Life was not too exciting at this point. I spent most of my days upstairs in the bedroom with Lily. Mom made sure that we alternated our times outdoors so that when one of us was out, the other was able to stay with the baby. I watched my Lily as she nursed our little girl. She was now beginning to look like a normal kid. Hahaha. I always teased Lily about this strange little creature that she gave birth to because she sure didn't look like either one of us.

Lily would giggle and just sit quiet again with her womanly wisdom neatly tucked away, not willing to share one bit of it. She amazed me. Here was this delicate, beautiful female who had gone through a hell-raising experience. She was brutally kicked, gave birth and survived the death of two of her children and she still managed to be warm and loving with a twinkle in her eye every day. Every day I loved her more and more.

Each morning Baby would get down on her hands and knees and take a quick peek at all of us. She would stroke our little girl with one finger and then she'd kiss Lily and kiss me and then go about her day. Mom would come up a few times during the day to make sure Lily and child were doing okay.

One day I heard Baby talking to Mom.

"Mom, we haven't decided on a name for the puppy yet? What should we call her?"

"Well, I don't know, honey. Let's think about this. Does she remind you of anything or anybody?"

"No, not exactly."

"We can't tell if she has any special characteristics at this point. But you know what? Her color is starting to come in."

"Yeah, it is! She kind of reminds me of a coconut. She has the color of a coconut and then she has these little speckles all around her that looks like flakes of coconut."

"Well, then, how about if we call her Coconut?"

"Oh, I like that! And I think she will, too!"

"Alright then. Coconut it is."

"I'm going to run upstairs and tell JoJo and Lily. I think they'll love it, too."

Baby ran up to us right away to deliver the news. Lily and I just looked at one another, not quite sure as to whether or not we liked it. But then we started saying it over and over and you know what? We liked it! So Coconut she became. Our little Coconut. Our baby.

Life had become pretty quiet although there still was not a big connection any more between Mom and Dad. We lived our lives kind of separate from each other. Oh, we were taken care of fine. We had plenty of food and water and we got out to do our business. We had some playtime with Baby. By now, Coconut was getting around and loving her playtime outside, too. But for the most part, we all stayed together and didn't really interact with the rest of the family.

## JoJo: A Dog's Tale

One night when we all were going downstairs to go outside with Baby, Mom and Dad were sitting at the kitchen table. The conversation was stilted and the news was not good.

"Brad, I don't think this is going to work. I think we need to go our separate ways and put this all behind us. I don't want this kind of life and I don't want our child to have to live through this. Let's try and work out an agreement."

"Whatever. I'm through trying."

"Trying? Trying? What on earth have you tried to do? You haven't tried anything. All you've done is what you usually do. And that is take no responsibility for your actions and point the finger at everybody else because YOU can't make it work for yourself. Let's not even discuss this thing. Let's just make plans for disbanding this whole set-up and do it as easily as possible."

"Do what you have to do. I'm outta here."

"Oh, are you going to go out on one of your jaunts? Instead of face up to what we have to do, you're just going to run out again?"

"Yeah, I'm gonna run out. See ya'."

And out he went. Out the door, in the car, out the garage and off he went to do whatever it is that he does when he goes out like that.

A few hours later he returned. Smelling, stumbling, you know the whole routine. I happened to be in the kitchen with Mom when he came through the door. He stumbled in and made a beeline towards me. He stood over me, hands on hips.

"You know, you little fart, I think you have a lot to do with this mess! I think she's choosing you over me. How about that?"

He bent over and picked me up by my tail. He lifted me over his head and let me just hang there dangling in the air.

Ouch! Ouch! Oh, it hurt!

*Yip! Yip! Yip! Arf! Arf!* I barked and whined as loud as I could.

Oh, it was hurting real bad. My tail, my whole bottom of the tail and around my butt. Oh, OW!

"Put him down! Put him down now, you bastard! Put him down!"

"How about if I put him down across the yard? How's that?"

"Brad, if you hurt him any more I'm calling the police. Give him to me. Now!"

He finally brought me down out of the air and put me in Mom's arms. By this time, Baby and Lily were standing at the top of the stairs. Baby came running down.

"Darn you! Darn you! I hate you! I hate you! Why don't you leave?" She was pounding him as hard as she could.

Mom went for the stairs with me still in her arms, Lily right behind us and Baby taking up the rear. We went into Baby's bedroom and Mom closed the door. It was over for the night.

I could sense that there were some big changes in the air and I hoped and prayed that they would come soon. I tried sitting down but my butt and tail hurt too much so I sprawled out flat on my stomach next to Lily and Coconut.

"Oh, sweetie, are you okay? I know you must be in terrible pain."

"Oh, Lily, I'll be fine. Just need a few days for the tender spots to heal up. I'm just concerned that we all get out of this mess in tact. This is a nightmare."

"I know what you mean. I'm really frightened and I'm frightened for our little Coconut. That big brute can take all of us and toss us out to smithereens and who knowswhere or how we'll land. I sure hope Mom has a plan."

"Oh, I think she does. I've heard rumbles between her and Baby. And I think it's going to happen sooner than we think."

I could hear Dad in the bedroom throwing things around. He pulled a couple of big square bags out of an upper closet and started emptying his drawers and putting his clothes in the big bags.

Mom stood over him and watched. "What are you doing?"

"I'm packing and getting the hell out of here. You can do whatever you want."

"Brad, I cannot afford this place on my own. Are you going to just run out on us and leave this whole mess up to me?"

"Yup! That's exactly what I'm going to do. I thought putting this deal together was a good thing. Boy! Was I wrong!"

"There you go again blaming everyone else for your shortcomings. YOU are the one making our lives miserable with your drinking and carousing. Am I supposed to just sit here like the good little woman and let you run loose all over the city and county like a single man? How stupid do you think I am? Really, how desperate do you think I am?"

"I'm just thinking about getting out. This whole thing was a big mistake."

"Well, what am I supposed to do? Aren't you even going to talk to the landlord?"

"Nope."

"You know what? Go. Just pack and go and don't ever look back. When you are drunk you are inconceivably ridiculous in your thinking and logic. If there is any logic at all in that sick brain of yours. Good bye, Brad. Have a nice life."

"Yeah, you, too."

He closed the bags, lifted them off the bed and out he went. I was sad. We were all sad. It all started out to be a dream come true and it turned into the worst nightmare we could have ever thought. But through it all, we all survived. And now, our next move was up to Mom. We were all ready to face whatever was in front of us as long as we were all together.

The ugly truth of it all was yet to come.

## Chapter 15

The next couple of days were a blur. Mom and Baby were in and out of the house. Boxes came in and boxes went out. Some of the small things that they had moved in were being taken out of the house little by little. I wasn't really sure what was happening but I was convinced that whatever it was was in the best interest of all of us. Mom would make sure of that.

Then, the worst day of my life was upon us. Lily and Coconut and I were downstairs in the living room just laying on the carpet looking out the window. I could hear Baby upstairs seemingly having a fit. She was screaming and crying but I couldn't really make out what she was saying. They were too far away and she was having difficulty getting her words out in between her tears and sobs and gasps for air. But then I heard Mom.

"Honey, it's going to be okay. They'll be fine. I've called the landlord and told him we're leaving and he should come by the house in a day or two. We'll leave enough food and water and blankets. They'll be fine for a day or two."

"But Mom, why can't we take them with us? We love them so. Why can't they come?"

"Sweetie, it takes a long time to find an apartment that will take pets. One that we can afford. We don't have that kind of time. We have to leave now. Trust me, they'll be fine."

"Can't we put them somewhere and then come back to get them?"

"We don't have anywhere to put them. A kennel is way too expensive for us now, so we'll just have to leave them. Now that's final. Let's not dwell on it. Get your things and let's go."

What on earth were they saying? Were they leaving? For good? Did they say they were leaving us? Where? Where were they leaving us? Oh god, what's going on?

Mom and Baby came downstairs with coats in hand and a few bags of stuff. They put them down near the front door and began to make their way towards us. We all just sat.

Baby picked up Coconut and Mom put leashes on me and Lily.

"Come on, boys and girls. We have to go now. Follow me."

She headed toward the basement door and opened it. She started down the stairs with Lily and I following on the leashes. What's happening? Where are we going and why?

We reached the bottom of the stairs and over in the corner was a batch of blankets piled in a heap. Next to them was a big bowl of water and two bowls of food. Looked like enough for a couple of days. A couple of darks. What does this mean?

"Okay, kids, this is it. We love you, but we can't take you with us. You be good guys and someone will come in a day or two."

Baby came over and got down on her knees. I was very confused. Lily was confused. We just looked at one another. Baby reached over to touch us and then she kissed each of us on the nose.

"Bye, JoJo. Bye, Lily. Bye, my little Coconut. Oh, Mom, I can't leave them."

She started to sob and Mom reached over and picked her up and led her to the stairs. She turned and looked back.

"I love you, my little puppies. I love you, don't ever forget that. I love you!"

And up the stairs they went and closed the door behind them. There was no light except for the daylight that came through the small windows that were way up on top of the walls. The air was damp and chilly, but thank goodness, we had the blankets. Lily and I rustled around the blankets and made a little nest and settled in.

"JoJo, what's happening?"

"Well, my sweet, I think we have just been left behind. Left to fend for ourselves. Let's hope it truly is only going to be a day or two."

We put our heads down next to one another and nuzzled noses. Our only comfort at this point was each other. Coconut busied herself running around the basement floor getting into each nook and cranny that she could find. Then she stopped and made a puddle. Hey, what else was she going to do. It was clear that there wasn't going to be anyone to take us out for a day or two so we just had to make do.

Lily and I closed our eyes and tried to catch a little nap. I knew her head was spinning just like mine. There was a whirlwind of questions swirling around in there. Questions with no answers. Coconut was tired of her exploration and came over with us and lay down.

An hour or so later, we all opened our eyes and looked around. Nothing had changed. I was a little hungry but told Lily and Coconut to go ahead and eat something before I did. I wanted to make sure they were taken care of first. They ate and drank some water and came back over to the blanket. Then I went and ate a little but I didn't have much of an appetite. It was beginning to get dark as we could tell by the diminishing light from the windows.

This was a waiting game. And the worst game I ever played. We were waiting for new humans. We were waiting to be taken somewhere else. We were waiting to find out what our future would be. Then the ugly reality of it all began to slowly creep inside me. I choked a little not wanting to let Lily know that there was a very deep concern that was hovering over us.

This concern was something that I had learned from Big Dog and along with that concern was a word that no dog ever wants to hear. A concern with the reality that no dog ever wants to face. Don't tell me that it had become a part of our life. Don't tell me that we were facing this nightmare. I didn't want to believe it and I didn't want to have it exposed to my Lily and my little Coconut. But there it was rearing its ugly face right before us. That word. That concern. That reality. And it all came down to one thing. One horrible, frightening existence. And that thing, that reality, was *rescue*. We were waiting to be . . . *rescued!*

*JoJo: A Dog's Tale*

## Chapter 16

We all managed to make it through the first dark and slowly began to open our eyes as the sun peeped its first glow through the upper windows. Although my sleep was restless, to be sure, it looked like Lily and Coconut had experienced a good, sound sleep.

Coconut was the first one to search the area for a spot to relieve herself. It was a big basement and we could tell that there was certainly plenty of room. Then I let Lily do her own search and I followed suit. The next thing on our minds was a nice cool drink of water, always the best first thing in the morning.

My mind was reeling with uncertainty and I was ever so fearful that Lily was going to start throwing questions at me. Again, questions that I had no answers for. We plunked ourselves back down on the blankets and pondered the day's activity. Who was I kidding? There was going to be no activity. No one to play with. No one to walk us. No one to talk to us. No one to do anything. We were alone. And that's how we were going to spend our day, or maybe two days. Pretty dreary outlook, to say the least.

Later in the day, we all got a little hungry and made our way to the bowls to eat. I tried to estimate how much food we had between the three of us and how long it would last. I thought we were in pretty good shape considering that our wait was to be two days at the most and it looked like we would have enough food and water for at least four days. Okay, I could live with that.

Lily and I sat quietly as we watched Coconut exercise her right to curiosity. She spent most of the morning just snooping around smelling and even pulling on a few things here and there. But even her curiosity wasn't enough to hold her interest all day. Eventually, she got bored and came over by us and lay down again. She closed her eyes and took her nap. Lily and I tried to do the same but somehow our anxiety was getting the best of us.

The boredom, certainly, was something to overcome if that was at all possible. But compounded with uncertainty, it made the day harder. If we had something to keep us busy, perhaps our thoughts wouldn't be completely overwhelmed with worry and anxiety. But we had nothing to keep us busy and as a result, our thoughts were overwhelmed with worry and anxiety!

We spent the rest of the day just hanging about, eating, drinking and watching Coconut. The dark was approaching again so we made the best of it and closed our eyes. I needed sleep badly and hoped that the veil of rest would envelop me. No such luck. Another restless night.

As we approached the third day, my heart began to skip a beat here and there. Every sound I heard from the outside I was sure was going to find its way inside. I waited for doors to open, footsteps to find there way across the floor above. I waited for voices to echo through the empty rooms and find a way to wrap around us. None of that happened. No doors opened, no footsteps pounded across the floors, no voices. This went on all day and through the next dark. And again, another day and another dark. And again, another day and another dark.

I lost count. I looked at our bowls. The water was down to just a lap or two. The food was almost completely gone. Where are the humans that are supposed to be finding us? No, excuse me. Let me reword that. Where are the humans that are supposed to be *rescuing* us?

Yes, there it was! The reality! We were in a dire and desperate situation. We were in need of rescue! How harsh it sounded when you are encompassed by the reality of it. How forlorn and dark the word is when you're on the wrong side of the fence.

As the days and darks continued on, I could hear the growling in my little Coconut's stomach. I could hear the growling in all of our stomachs, but my main concern was Coconut.

"Dad? I'm hungry."

"I know, baby, I know. We're all hungry. Just hold on a little longer. I'm sure some food is coming soon."

"I'm thirsty, too."

"I know, Coconut. Just hang on."

We repeated that conversation all day every day until Coconut really didn't care any more. She placed herself next to Lily and just lay there all day. Lily was in no better shape. We were all in bad shape. No food. No water. And none of us had any energy to even walk across the floor. How long had it been? Nine days? Ten days? Didn't know anymore. Didn't care. I thought of Big Dog. I could really use some help now, but Big Dog was gone. He was over the Rainbow Bridge. He was gone.

"Hey kid, no I ain't? I'm not all gone."

"Big Dog, is that you? Am I dreaming?"

"No, kid, you're not dreaming. It's me alright. I told you we could still talk. Don't you remember when I told you?"

"Yeah, I think I do."

"Listen, I know the situation you're in. I'm here to tell you that everything is going to be alright."

"How can you say that? How do you know?"

"Trust me, I know. Over here we know a lot about a lot of things."

"Well, if it's going to happen, it better happen soon. None of us can walk. We have no food, we have no water . . . and I'm afraid that we just might be looking at the Rainbow Bridge ourselves."

"No, kid, no, you ain't. Hang on, kid. You're tough. You're a warrior, remember? A real warrior!"

"Yeah, I remember. I remember . . ."

After that I drifted off to sleep again. We slept a lot these days. We didn't have the energy to do much else. I looked at Lily and Coconut and they were barely breathing. I nudged over to Lily and nuzzled her nose. She nuzzled back as best she could.

"I'm still here with you, my love."

"I know, JoJo. I know."

We both just lay there and closed our eyes and just waited. We waited. We listened. Nothing. Day after day there was silence. My ears began to hurt because I listened so hard.

Suddenly, I thought I did hear something! I opened my eyes and lifted my head ever so slightly. I was so weak I could barely move. Yes! I did hear something. There it was again!

Click! Bump! Bang! Clop clop! Oh my god, someone was in the house. I needed to let them know we were here! I needed to bark! I needed to move! I needed to get to the top of the stairs and to that door! How in Sky Dog's name was I going to do that?

Warrior! Warrior! I heard it over and over again in my head. I heard Big Dog. Warrior! I was a warrior! I pulled myself up with my shaking legs and began to drag myself over to the stairs. I lifted my one leg up, then the next, then the next and slowly, inch by inch began to make my way up the stairs. I took a deep breath and gathered every ounce of strength I could muster up. *Yip! Yip! Arf! Yip!*

"Help! Help! Oh god, somebody help us! Please! We need help!" I had to stop. I couldn't do both. I couldn't drag myself up and bark at the same time. I moved up a few more steps and started again. *Yip! Yip!*

"Help! Help! My baby needs water! Help!" I knew I had to be the strength and the power if anything was going to happen. If there was any chance at all that we would be saved, it would have to be because I wouldn't give up. I was a warrior! Warriors don't give up. *Yip! Yip!*

And then, there it was! The door to the basement opened! Oh god, there he was! Our rescuer! He stepped down a step or two to reach down and grab me. I couldn't let that happen. I needed to get him all the way down so he could see Lily and Coconut were down here, too.

I moved back down two steps. He came down those same two steps and reached down again. I moved down another two steps. He came down again. We continued this all the way down onto the floor and I clumsily walked over to where Lily and Coconut were laying.

"Oh my god! Teresa, get down here now!" He shouted back up the stairs.

"Why? What's going on?"

"Just get down here. And bring one of those big boxes with you."

I could hear a scuffling up on the floor and then more footsteps coming down the stairs. A beautiful lady walked over to us and put down this big box.

"Oh my goodness, what do we have here?"

"Well, it looks like our last tenants left us some of their belongings. No wonder she was so adamant that I get here in a day or two. If she would have only told me, I would have. But I had other properties to take care of and figured I could get to this one later. Oh god, I hope they're all alright. Look, let's put one of these blankets in the box, get them all in there and over to Dr. Ward's office right away. Get on the phone and tell him we're on our way over with three pups

## JoJo: A Dog's Tale

that are in really bad shape. Looks like starvation and dehydration. C'mon, let's get going."

They picked us all up and placed us in the box. I could feel those water droplets in my eyes again along with an overwhelming feeling of thankfulness. We were safe. Coconut was safe. Lily was safe. We had been *rescued!* Lily opened her eyes just slightly. She was so weak.

"Lily! Lily, darling! Hang on, my sweet. It's going to be alright. We've been found. We're going to be fine!"

"Really? Really, JoJo?"

"Yes, oh yes, we're going to be fine."

"I knew you'd save us. You are my warrior."

And she closed her eyes again and took a deep breath and nestled into safety. Yes, she was going to be fine. And Coconut! Little Coconut was going to be fine. We were all going to fine!

Was this another new beginning? Or was this the beginning of another end? I didn't know. I . . . didn't know. I crossed my paws and hoped for the best.

*JoJo: A Dog's Tale*

## Chapter 17

All of us had drifted off into a restful dream-like state. Our energy had been completely depleted and none of us had the ability to even lift our heads and look about. We just lay on the blanket inside the big box. I could tell that we were taken outside because as I looked upward with my eyes, I could see the tops of trees and the blue sky. Yes, we were really out of the dark basement and out into the fresh air again. That was certainly a good thing, but where we were going, we did not know and that was not a good thing.

But for now, my only concern was getting better and feeling better and certainly I was concerned about Lily and Coconut. They were really my top priority at this point. I looked over at little Coconut and I prayed that her closed eyes only meant that she was exhausted and also depleted of energy and that those closed eyes didn't mean something more serious.

"Coconut. Coconut. Can you hear me?"
"Huh? Huh? Dad? Is that you?"
Her little eyes squeezed open just a bit.
"Yes, honey, it's me. Are you okay?"
"I'm real tired, Dad."

"I know, honey, I know. Hang on, you're going to be just fine."

"Okay. But I'm real sleepy."

"That's okay. Just keep your mind busy. Think of all the toys you used to play with and the games we used to play in the backyard."

"Okay, Dad. Okay."

Her breathing seemed to get a little fuller and she moved her little legs a bit here and there. I knew she was going to be fine. She was just like her Dad. A warrior.

"Lily? Lily, how are you feeling?"

"I'll be fine. I'm tired, too, but I'll be fine. Just to know that we're safe has made me feel much better."

"Yeah, me, too. Just stay with me and think good things."

"I will, JoJo. I will."

We all clung together, each one touching this one or that one, each one looking for reassurance that this was really happening and wasn't just a dream. Yes, we were actually safe.

Our rescue man put our box in the back of his car as carefully as he could. I could feel lots of kindness coming from him and his partner. I could tell that they were good humans.

He started the car and off we went. I know it probably took several minutes to get to where we needed to go, but in our drifting state of consciousness, it seemed like just a minute or two. We arrived at a building and our rescue man immediately stopped the car in front, jumped out of his seat and came around to get our box. He picked us up and just literally ran into the building.

"Dr. Ward! Dr. Ward!" he screamed. "Get Dr. Ward immediately!"

The other people in the room ran to the back and returned with another man with a silver thing around his neck. He came right over to our box and put the silver thing against little Coconut's chest.

"This one's weak but she'll be fine. Get them all set up for intravenous feeding. Looks like they're going to need some immediate hydration."

He continued to put the silver thing to my chest and then to Lily's chest.

"This one here is the weakest. Let's move fast."

He was talking about Lily! Oh my god, my Lily.

"Lily! Lily! Hang on, my sweet, hang on."

"I . . . I'm trying JoJo. I'm trying."

"Lily, hang one. I'm here. Coconut's here. And Coconut is going to be fine. Did you hear me? Coconut is okay!"

"Oh, I'm so relieved."

"Lily, hang on."

By now there were several people around. Our rescue man was still standing with us.

"Listen, Doc, you do whatever you have to do to save these little guys, you hear me?"

"You bet, Stan. Don't worry, we're going to do our best."

Our box was lifted again and we were taken to the back room. It was stark and it was very, very white with lots of big lights. Two ladies lifted us out of the box and onto a table. There was nothing we could do but simply lay there. But somehow, I trusted this bunch. Somehow I knew their only concern was to save us and make us all better.

As we lay still, they began to move all kinds of strange and foreign equipment towards us. I was still confident and didn't feel one inch of fear. They started sticking us with very small silver pins connected to tubes. Each one of us was connected to two bottles filled with some kind of liquid. But it was still okay. Yes, I knew it was going to be okay.

I think Coconut was the first one to drift off to sleep, then Lily, then me. I knew that was the order because I had kept my eye on both of them during the whole set-up process. I forced myself to stay awake because I wanted to be there if they had questions or if they just needed me to be there. But now that everyone had been taken care of, I could close my eyes and rest peacefully. I nudged over to Lily and nuzzled her nose.

"Oh, look at this one! How cute is he?", one of the ladies had noticed me moving over to Lily.

"He wants to be near his lady. How adorable."

Yeah, how adorable, I thought. All of us were on death's door, you know, Rainbow Bridge material, and they think we're adorable. We must be really cute when we're feeling good! But in my heart, I thanked them for their caring and their kindness. Big Dog was right, as usual. There are good ones and there are bad ones. We certainly experienced some of the bad ones. But Sky Dog was with us because now we were among the good ones. My hope was that our luck would continue. But at this point, I wasn't sure. I just wasn't sure anymore.

*JoJo: A Dog's Tale*

## Chapter 18

"Dad! Dad! Wake up! Dad!"

It was Coconut. Her eyes bright and her tail wagging and her tongue licking my nose with great determination!

"Wha..? What?"

"Dad, wake up! Where are we?"

I slowly opened my eyes and blinked a few times while Coconut was still making mince-meat out of my nose.

"Slow down, there, kiddo! Relax! I don't know exactly where we are, but we're in a good place. How are you feeling?"

"I feel fine. Where's Mom? Dad, where's Mom?"

I looked around. Lily was nowhere to be seen. Oh my god, where is she? Where is Lily?

"Lily? Lily? Where are you? Where are you?"

"I'm right here, JoJo. I'm in the next room. The ladies are taking out my silver pins and wiping my eyes. I'm fine. Just fine."

Whew! Did I just have the scare of my life or what? So much had happened and the changes were coming fast.

"Mom is fine, Coconut. She's just in the next room. She'll be back in a few minutes."

Just then, the door opened and here they all came. The ladies, the man and Lily. My goodness, she looked great! She looked rested and comfortable.

"Lily, you look fabulous!"

"Thanks, hon. I feel pretty good. I think both of you are going in next. But don't worry. They are all very, very nice. Very caring humans."

Just then, one of the ladies reached over for Coconut.

"Dad! Dad! Where am I going? Where are they taking me?"

"Calm down, Coconut. They're just taking you into the next room to clean you off and take out your silver pins. You'll be fine."

It took just a few mintues for Coconut and then it was my turn. It was amazing how one day and one dark can make such a difference. I don't know what those liquids were that were flowing in us all night, but it sure made a difference. We were rested and our energy had returned. Not full blast, just yet, but I could certainly tell the difference. We were beginning to feel frisky! And my past experience was telling me that frisky was good!

The only thing that upset me a little was the fact that we were all in a cage. Another cage, much like the one I had come from. I thought Lily might be familiar with it, but Coconut sure didn't have any idea what a cage was. It was comfortable enough and very clean. But nonetheless, a cage.

I saw the door to the room open and two of the ladies were coming through with bowls in their hands. Oh my, it was real food and real water. They opened the door to the cage and put the bowls inside with us. Of course, Coconut was the first one to dash over and start gobbling and slurping.

"Hey, slow down a bit there, little one. You don't want to make yourself sick."

It was a fruitless effort. She hadn't really seen any food for almost ten or eleven days. How could I stop her or control her. Actually, why did I want to? It was a delight to have the food and a delight to watch her enjoy it.

Having filled her little belly, which by now was blorping out a bit, she turned and settled into a corner. I could tell that she overdid it and now needed to just lie down and digest, the little piggy. Lily and I made our way over to the bowls and just stood for a minute. We glanced at one another, nuzzled noses, and began to eat, each one of us saying a silent prayer of thanks to Sky Dog for watching over us and making sure we were safe. Lily and I also filled ourselves, drank a little water, and moved over to the corner to join Coconut. We were all well and we were all safe. We had had a good night's sleep and had some good food and plenty of water. What else did we need?

We needed plenty. We needed some new humans and a new Forever Home! I wasn't going to settle for this cage. Something had to happen and something needed to be done. But reality hit again. Whatever is was that needed to be done was completely and totally out of my control. All we could do is hope that something was going to happen that would change our current existence.

The rest of the day was spent just resting up and every now and then one of the ladies would come by to check our food and water bowls. It seemed to be a never-ending supply. A far cry from the last two weeks when we were left with enough food and water for four days. Ouch. I can't bear to think of those days. I will have nightmares for years to come, I'm sure. For now, I just wanted to focus on the future.

We hadn't seen our rescue man, but the other man from this building, the one who walked around with the silver thing that he would put to our chest, had come around once or twice. He gave us a quick look, a quick pet, and a quick tweek on the ear. He was nice. He was good.

The dark was coming and we were all getting a little sleepy. Coconut drifted off first. Lily and I did our usual nuzzle and we both drifted off to sleep. I was concerned about what the following day was going to bring and what new experience we would be confronted with. Little did I know that there would be continous movement and activity for all of us in the coming days. I was hoping that Lily and Coconut were not going to be inquisitive and would be content to just nestle in for the time-being. If they had questions, I was in big trouble. Again, I had no answers.

*JoJo: A Dog's Tale*

## Chapter 19

The following morning found us all just lazing our way to opening our eyes. No one was in a particular hurry to wake up, but we weren't sound asleep any more either. I think the past few weeks had taken its toll and we were all just thankful and grateful to be where we were. Not that we were savoring any of our surroundings, of course, but it was a darn sight better than what we had just come from. It wasn't heaven, but it would do.

We heard some activity outside the door and several voices were sounding. They were a bit muffled because of the closed door but then one of the ladies opened the door and several people came walking into our room.

"Well, lookee here, what do we have before us?"

"Looks like a whole family to me!"

"Yeah, Henry, I think you're right. And a bunch of cuties, to be sure."

"Well, let's get them scooped up and on our way. We've got a couple more stops to make before we call it a day."

With that, they began to reach into our cage and make a grab for us. Not menacing, but these were strange men. Who are they? Where did they come from? And more importantly, where were they taking us? I snapped and growled. So did Lily. Coconut just sat there looking confused.

"Oh my, looks like we've got a couple of little toughies on our hands. Henry, got get those muzzles. I think we've got a couple that are small enough."

"Right. Be back in a sec."

Muzzles! What are muzzles? What is he talking about?

The other guy returned almost immediately and came in holding these strange looking things and he had a long stick with a loop on the end of it. What th . . .? What was going on?

The other guy took the stick with the loop on it and reached it into the cage. He managed to loop it around my neck and pulled me to the cage door. I didn't struggle and I didn't growl or bite. My instinct was telling me that if I did all of that I was just going to make it worse for myself. He reached up with this thing that he slipped over my jaw and nose and snapped it in the back. I couldn't move my jaw. I couldn't open my mouth. I sure couldn't bark much less bite anybody. So, this was a muzzle. I probably looked pretty stupid.

"Let's see if we can get the second one here."

Lily saw the muzzle that they had placed on me and she, in her wisdom, just quietly walked over to the cage door and stood there.

"I don't think we're going to have a problem with this one. She seems pretty calm. And the little one, for sure, is okay. Does anybody know what their names are?"

One of the ladies came up to the cage.

"The guy who brought them in said he found a note in the house. They were all left abandoned in the basement after the people who were the renters moved out. The note said that the male was named JoJo, the big female is Lily, and the little one is Coconut."

"Well, I'll be. Ain't they just the cute ones. And what great names."

The same lady started to speak again.

"Listen, let me hold the male, little JoJo, and see if we can get this muzzle off. I really don't think he needs it. I think he was just scared of you guys when you came in and stormed into his cage. You have to understand what they've gone through."

"Go ahead, little lady. I'm not a mean guy and I sure don't want to have to put those things on them if it ain't necessary. Hey, I might be big and burly . . . "

"I know, I know, but inside you're a real pussycat."

"You got it! I'm a pushover for these little guys. I get my heart broken a hundred times a day. It's a good thing I live in a very small house else I'd be taken a few home with me every day."

The lady picked me up and started to remove my muzzle. I'm not stupid. I sat still and didn't make a sound. When she finally got it off, I licked her hand. Twice.

"See. He was just afraid."

"Here, let me see if I can handle him."

He reached over and picked me out of her arms and let me nestle in his big shirt. I just lay very quiet.

"There ya' go, little fella. See, I knew we'd get along fine if we just gave each other a chance."

Yeah, he was good. He was one of the good ones, too.

"See, lady, us guys here with Animal Control aren't the bad guys. It's the ones who mistreat these babies that are the bad guys. You'd be surprised how many of our workers actually do take some of these guys home. And we have girls back at the facility who get in touch with various organizations to try and get these little ones adopted out to good homes."

Oh my goodness! It was actually happening! We were being given a second chance. A chance for a new life. New humans. A new Forever Home. I could hardly contain myself. In fact, I didn't. I peed.

"Oh my, lookee here! We got a little piddle goin' on! Hahaha! I sure hope that ain't cuz he's scared. I'm sure not tryin' to scare this little guy. Whatever, we'll just deal with it."

They gently put us all in a smaller cage that they could lift and move around. Then they carried the cage out to a big truck and opened the back end of it. I couldn't believe my eyes.

"Hey, hey, how are you doing? Where did you come from?"

"What's your name?"

"Are these your friends?"

I was being slammed with a million questions from a very large group of dogs that had been caged and put in the back of the truck. All different colors, all different size, all different cages. Were they abandoned, too? Were they waiting for new Forever Homes, too? Would there by enough for all of us?

Questions, questions and more questions. As usual, I had no answers.

*JoJo: A Dog's Tale*

# Chapter 20

Lily, Coconut and I were somewhat dazed. We didn't particularly feel any hostilities coming from anywhere or anyone. But there was an overlying uncertainty that prevailed over all of us, including our new found friends here in the back of the truck.

"So we just wanted to say hello. How are you guys doing?"

"Oh, we seem to be doing okay, I guess." I answered my inquisitive new friend.

"Well, I'm Muffie. That's Daisy, that's Big George, Ginger over there, Duke, Tinker and Buster."

"Pleased to meet you all, I guess. I'm JoJo. This is Lily and that's our little Coconut."

"Hey."

"Hey."

"So where'd you come from?"

"Well, several places, actually. Where would you like me to start?"

"Oh, never mind. I'm sure we've all got a familiar story."

"More importantly, where are we going?" I wasn't really sure I wanted to hear the answer to that question.

The bigger one in the back started to answer.

"I think we're headed to the Animal Control facility. It's not too bad there. All the folks are really kind and caring and there's always plenty of food and plenty of other dogs to talk to."

"What exactly happens there?"

"Not much. We all just sort of hang out until something happens. Either our owners come and get us, or a new group comes for us, or new humans come for us, or, if none of that happens, then we go to the City Shelter and get zipped."

*Zipped?* There was that word again.

"What do you mean zipped?" Again, I didn't really want to ask because I really didn't want to get the answer I was expecting.

"You know, the Rainbow Bridge thing."

How many times in my life do I have to deal with this "Rainbow Bridge thing." Eventually, we'll all get there, I know, but to be confronted with it at every other turn was getting depressing, to say the least.

I looked at Lily and she had heard and understood everything that was being said. I could tell that she wasn't afraid, but she was getting very, very sad looking.

"Lily, please don't be sad."

"Oh, JoJo, I just want all of us to be happy. I want all of us to be safe and secure and in a place where we don't have to worry any more, that's all."

"I know, honey. I want the same thing for us. For all of us. But something tells me that we're going to be okay. I've got a feeling in my bones that tells me so."

"I'm sure you do. You always manage to make things right for us."

Well, talk about putting a huge responsibility on one's shoulders. *I always manage to make things right.* I wasn't really feeling that. So far, it felt like I always managed to screw things up. But truth be told, I knew that I really had no control over anything that had happened to us up to now. Not the good things, not the bad things. None of it. And here we were again in a situation that I didn't get us into and had no clue of how I was going to get us out of it. Good going, JoJo.

The truck traveled through the streets turning and stopping and starting and turning. We chatted amongst us, just making small talk. I think everyone was apprehensive at this point. There was a lot of sighing going on and shaking of heads but we all just hung together and tried to make the best of it.

The truck finally stopped and the doors to the back opened wide. There were several other people standing there, each one ready to assist with the cages in the truck. Each cage was carefully lifted and carted inside a building, down a hallway and into a huge room with hundreds of other cages. I could hear barking and yipping and whining. This was not a good feeling. Lily, Coconut and I were separated from the other dogs that we made the trip with and we were taken to yet another room and our cage was put down somewhere in the middle. Then all of the people disappeared and left us alone in the room. There were several other cages in with us. I looked around trying to get a feel for what was happening.

"Say, I'm JoJo. Have you been here long?" I tried to connect with the guy in the next cage.

"Oh, I've been here about three darks, I guess. This is what they call the Short Term Area here."

Oh oh. That also did not sound good.

"What exactly is a Short Term Area?"

"Oh, that's just where they put you if they have other plans for you and don't expect you to be here long."

"Like, what other plans." I choked a little and waited for my heart to make it back down out of my throat.

"Well, you and your crew there look pretty pedigree so I'm assuming they're going to try and hook you up with a group that will take you. I, myself, got hooked up with a special group for my breed. They're just waiting to find a foster home for me and then I'm outta here."

"Foster home? What's a foster home?"

"Oh, it's a home that you go to with some people that will care for you and feed you and all that stuff until they can find a permanent home for you."

"You mean . . . you mean a . . . Forever Home?"

"Hey, yeah, that's it! A Forever Home."

My knees almost buckled out from under me. A Forever Home! We were actually headed for another Forever Home! I started trembling with joy. I looked at Lily as she began to move closer to me. She nuzzled me. I nuzzled back.

"It's okay, JoJo, it's okay."

She pressed hard against me comforting me. She knew I was at my emotional end. I whined a tiny whine, a whine of joy, if you will. She licked my nose and nuzzled me again. She could see the relief all over my body. Mind you, I was never scared for myself. It was my beautiful mate and my darling puppy child that was my biggest, my only concern. To know that they were really going to be safe and secure meant the world to me. I finally let my knees take me down and I just crumbled to the bottom of the cage. Lily came right down with me. The two of us just lay next to one another squeezing tighter and tighter into each other. It was finally over. At least, almost over. We both closed our eyes and pictured a beautiful home with a great Mom and Dad who would love us with all their might. We pictured toys and food and fluffy beds and great mornings with the smell of breakfast cooking and morning kisses and hugs. But, alas, as wonderful as it played before us, our fabulous dream picture was shattered with another stark reality.

"Hey Dad, I'm hungry!"

*JoJo: A Dog's Tale*

# Chapter 21

We sat in our cages for quite some time before anybody came to see us. My little Coconut was complaining the whole time about being hungry which was her usual state, so this was nothing unusual. I'm told they will eat you out of house and home if you let them.

Finally, the doors opened and in walked another big, burley sort of a man. My instant reaction was to protect my family.

"Grrrrrrrr!" I wasn't sure what he had on his mind, but I wasn't going to give in without a fight.

"What's up there, little guy? What are you so cranky about?" The big burly moved in closer.

"Grrrrrrr!" I made myself as fierce as I could. Not that my five pounds and ten inches could scare a gnat, but I sure gave it my best. I wondered what he would do if I snapped at him.

But then, what was that? I smelled something. It was food! Oh my goodness, big burly was bringing us food. He was here to give us our dinner. Oh great, JoJo. Almost screwed up another moment in time.

He opened our cage and slid in three full bowls of food. Coconut went after hers like no tomorrow. I just stood still to make sure Lily could get herself over to her bowl and start eating. Instead, she walked over to me and just stood looking at me.

"What?" I asked.

"I just wanted to say thank you for being so brave on our behalf. You are truly a wonderful protector."

"Aww, just tryin' to do my job."

"Well, thank you, again. Are you going to eat?"

"As soon as you do."

"Okay. I'm feeling much better, thanks to you."

"Don't thank me too much, my Lily. We still don't know what the future holds."

"I know, but you've been our strength up to now."

She turned and went over to her bowl and started to dip into it. Just then, Coconut, after wolfing down every morsel from his own dish, moved over to Lily's bowl, growled at her, and began to start on her food.

"Hey! What's with you?" I screamed.

"I'm hungry!"

"We're all hungry, but you've had yours. Settle down and let your mother eat."

Coconut slowly moved away from Lily's bowl and went to lie down in the corner of the cage.

I started to eat, but watched over Lily and her bowl just to make sure that Coconut didn't try to sneak her way over. I finished most of mine, but left a little in the bottom.

"Here, you can have what's left of mine. But don't ever do that again."

Coconut moved over very quietly to my bowl and began to gently finish off what was left. She had learned a lesson today and I know she will be better off for it. If she was going to get spoiled, it wasn't going to be on my account. In our current situation, this was not the time to start acting like a spoiled brat.

Finished with all our food, we just settled down for a good night's sleep. Hopefully, the morning light would bring good news for us and give us some idea of what was ahead for us.

Big burly came in to retrieve our empty bowls and put some fresh water in the cage for us.

"You little guys have a good night's sleep, you hear? We've got some new folks coming tomorrow to take a look at you to see where we can put you. You're a fine bunch, you are, and I think we're going to get some really nice homes for you."

New people? Nice homes? It sounded like heaven, alright. Although, we started out with a nice home in the beginning. It's funny how life can throw you a curve and pull the rug right out from under you. Here we were in this wonderful home with a good mom, a good dad, a great kid to play with. Then all of a sudden, everybody went crazy and the abuse started. I wasn't sure how much longer we'd be able to take the hits and the kicks. If they would have done anything to Lily or to Coconut, I would have had to have gone completely insane and jump for their throats! It's one thing to hurt me, but to hurt my beloved, hurt my child? No! That would have called for drastic measures.

Oh, who am I kidding? My five pounds wasn't going to hurt anybody. I guess it was just our fate to have been stashed away in the basement while everybody else just left. Abandoned. That's what we were. Simply abandoned. But a much better fate than to have to be stuck somewhere where physical abuse and neglect would have been the order of the day for who knows how long. Yes, being left was far better.

At least this way, we will have a second chance for a better life. A new life with new people. Somewhere there's a place for us. A place where love will be the order of the day.

Will this actually happen? Will we truly get a second chance? Will we be able to go from horrible to happy again? All we could do is hope upon hope that all these big burlys and these strange ladies were going to be a part of the puzzle. The pieces that put it all together. For me. For Lily. For Coconut.

Yes, all that was left was hope. And that alleged strength of mine that Lily was so proud of. As I lay my head down and started to drift off to sleep, one thought kept swirling around in my head, one phrase kept in the forefront of my thoughts. In my head, I said it over and over again until it engraved itself into my being.

*Be strong, JoJo. Be strong.*

## Chapter 22

The next morning we all awoke with a start. The doors banged open and a flurry of people walked through the doors. They started cleaning cages, changing water bowls, dropping off new bowls of food. It was busy and loud and rather joyful. Everyone seemed to be in a great mood and lots of talking and laughing. It felt good to have some decent positive vibes hanging around for a change.

All the dogs started barking. I'm not exactly sure why. I guess that's just what you do when you're in this situation. Some were barking for their food, which was on its way anyway. Some were barking because there were strangers in the room. And some were barking just to be barking. Lily and I didn't join in. We were still pretty tired from the previous days and weeks and just wanted to rest and catch up on our sleep and get our nerves in order.

After our cages were cleaned, we sauntered over to our food bowls and began to nibble a bit. Coconut, of course, was again wolfing down her food like they were going to un-invent the concept of food and she would never again see a single morsel. Strange creatures, these children dogs.

We spent most of the rest of the morning just lounging about the cage and having brief but friendly conversations with some of the other dogs. It was funny, but none of the other dogs seemed to be too concerned about their future. Somehow, they all knew that everything was going to be alright for them. Apparently, some of them had been through this process before and it didn't seem to phase them.

Their calm demeanor rubbed off on us because our nerves finally did calm down and we just lounged and napped. Briefly. Until the doors clanged open again.

"Well, here they are, the three of them. Not really sure what they're story is, but they all came in together. They're all pretty young and would make great pets for any family. Although, I doubt that a family would take all three of them. You'll probably have to split them up."

*What?* What did they say? Split us up? Oh god, no! We've come this far together and survived the pits of hell together and now they're going to split us up?

One of the other dogs chimed in. "Listen, kid, don't get so upset. You know, most families out there can't take three dogs at once. But these rescue places always make sure that the homes they put you in are absolutely the best places for you. And they keep checking on you and if it's just not the right place, they take you back and keep hunting until they find the perfect Forever Home."

"But . . . but . . . we've been through so much together!"

"I know, I know. But listen, there's a lot of us out here who have been through some hell, too. In a perfect world, it would be great if you could all stay together, but that's not likely to happen."

Just then, Lily was looking at me, her eyes filling with mist and water. Oh my Lily, what can I do to stop this? I can't. I'm being strong, but I can't control what's happening around us. She just slowly lay down and put her head down on her paws and closed her eyes. She knew what the outcome was going to be and she knew she couldn't fight it. Worse, she knew there wasn't one darn thing any of us could do about it. I walked over to her and lay next to her. I nuzzled her with my nose. She didn't even open one eye. She just sighed and nudged me with her body. We knew the end of "us" was coming and we just wanted to spend our last precious moments together in silence. A silence filled with love and pain. My throat got another lump in it and I held back my own eye mist and water.

The cage opened and a lady reached in to pick me up and out of the cage. She snuggled me close to her. She smelled good. She smelled like a nice lady.

"You know, I think I'll take all three of them with me. There's another rescue group that we work with that can probably find some great homes for the female and the baby. But for now, I'll take them all."

Was I hearing right? She was taking all of us? Wow! Was this great or what? Maybe, just maybe she'll decide to keep all of us. Maybe we do have a chance to go somewhere together.

"Listen, we have a doctor here today from the Waukesha humane association that performs neuters for the shelters very inexpensively. Would you like us to handle his neuter for you?"

Neuter? What's neuter? What are they talking about? They said 'his.' Does that mean me? What's neuter? "Hey, do any of you guys know what neuter is?" No answer. "Hey!" No answer.

Just then, I was picked up and carried into another room that was full of big, cold gray tables. They pulled out a blanket and tried to lay me down, but I wasn't going to have any of it. I struggled as best I could but there were some really big hands there. They didn't hurt me. Or hit me. They were just firm with me. I still wasn't having any of it!

I saw one of the ladies take something that looked very, very sharp and pointy with a small bottle at the end of it filled with some kind of liquid. She came at me and stuck it in my back thigh. Ouch. That smarted a bit! After that, they all stopped trying to lay me down and just stood there and looked at me.

I noticed that my legs were getting a little wobbly and my vision became blurred. I sat down and began to try and put all this action together and figure out what they were doing. But I was feeling too good to worry about those things right now. My head bobbed a little and I also noticed that my eyelids were getting a little heavy. I tried to stand up but gosh, I had no feeling in my legs and... hee hee... wow.

Yeah, I was feeling real good. All the ladies and men were just staring at me, smiling, and I was just sitting there... feeling... good...

*JoJo: A Dog's Tale*

# Chapter 23

Ow! Ooooo! What was that? I turned and felt a stabbing pain. Ouch! I opened my eyes and saw that I was back in my cage. Ooooo. Lily just lay there looking at me. She wasn't saying a word.

"Okay, anybody got any information on what just happened?"

"Hey kid, you've been under sedation."

It was one of the other dogs in the cage room.

"Sedation? What is sedation?"

"It's where they stick you with this pin and it puts you to sleep. Then they perform an operation on you."

"Operation? What kind of operation?"

"Welllll, it's kinda like this, kiddo. They remove parts of you so you can't make any more puppies."

"Oh that. I heard about that. *What?* You mean my parts are gone?!"

"Yup, all gone."

I wasn't sure how to take this. All I knew was that I had some strange looking little pieces of string stuck in me where my privates use to be and they were a bit "stingee" to say the least. It wasn't unbearable, but it was making moving around a little testy. I looked at Lily. She didn't seem too upset about things but yet she had this pensive look about her.

"Lily, are you okay? You're not looking too happy."

"Oh JoJo, I've learned that all of us are going to get the same operation. I'll be going soon and after that, I won't be able to have any more puppies either. I'm not really upset, just kind of sad about it. I'll be fine. The important thing is that you're okay and we get ourselves settled somewhere."

"Oh, my sweet, I'm so, so sorry."

"It's okay. I hear it happens to the best of us. They do that to those of us who end up in shelters or rescue places. They 'fix' us so we can't have any more puppies because then, if bad things happen to them, too, if there's too many of us, they wouldn't be able to find enough homes to take us. So, it's bad thing, but in the long run, it's a good thing. It's practical."

I nuzzled her with my nose and she nuzzled back. It was surely a puzzling and bittersweet time for us. On one hand, we knew we were safe. But on the other hand, we also knew that we would probably lose one another and lose Coconut. We would never see each other again and would have only our memories to live with. Hopefully, the journey from here on, would be a far better one than the last. My hopes were mainly for Lily and Coconut. I wanted them to be surrounded with love and care and to be spoiled with all the joys that life had to offer. Could this happen? Dare we ask Sky Dog again to grant us yet another wishful dream? Lily and I just snuggled together and savored the time we had left. Neither one of us knew what the future held. We just held on to each other. That night we slept closer to each other than we had ever done. We almost wrapped our legs and paws around each other. I could feel her breath on my chest and I knew she could feel my heart beating against hers. It was good, and it was not so good. It was still a bit frightful, but we felt a security that we had never felt before. We fell asleep and woke to the same morning activity as before. Happy people, happy sounds, happy, happy, happy. My hope was that all this happy could rub off on us and we could be as delirious as the rest of the group.

The doors opened and in came that same light haired lady from yesterday. She had this big cagey bag with her and reached into our cage, pulled me out, and put me in this big bag. Ouch! Ooooo! Owey! *Take it easy there, woman! I've got some stringees in my privates!*

Then she reached in and put a leash on Lily and Coconut, pulled them out and onto the floor as she held the other end of the leashes.

"Okay, little guys, let's get going. We've got some new moms and dads to find for you and get you all settled in some really good Forever Homes. So let's go!"

Lily and Coconut trotted out the door while the lady picked up the big bag with me in it and out we went into the world.

Yeah, out into the world! New moms and dads! New Forever Homes! What a sound! What a relief! It was true! It was happening! It was no longer a dream!

She put us into her automobile and off we went. She drove a while, but not a real long time. Then we pulled up and she parked the car. First, she took Lily and Coconut in and then she came back out to get me. She carried me in still inside the big bag. It was apparent that she knew I had these stringees in my privates and she didn't want me to walk too far. When we entered her house, she opened the bag and let me out. I limped out, my stringees and my privates still burning a little, but I was feeling much better.

I'm sure that my attitude and my state of mind had a lot to do with how my stringees and my privates were feeling. But I could tell that all was good now. Except for one thing.

"I'm Buddy. I live here. I own here. I'm number one here. Just so you know."

Oh brother, here we go again.

"I'm JoJo. Is this your Forever Home?"

"Yup. I own here. You're going to have to let me have first on everything. I'm Alpha."

I just rolled my eyes and sighed a deep sigh.

"Whatever." I wasn't in the mood to listen to this guy and all his rules and regulations about being Alpha and owning here, etc., etc. You wanna be Alpha? Be Alpha, I could care less.

I turned to see where Lily and Coconut were. Lily had found a comfy spot to rest her weary bones while Coconut began the scamper of the entire house. Usual kid stuff. I walked over to Lily.

"Lily, how are you feeling?"

"I'm fine. The big question is how are *you* feeling?"

"Oh, I'm okay. I'll be fine. You know, we gotta deal with Mr. Big Alpha over there."

## JoJo: A Dog's Tale

"Yes, I see that. Well, it *is* his home. And we are just visitors, so let's just give him his do and everything will be fine."

"Yeah, I guess you're right. We'll have our own places soon. Then we can run around screaming *Alpha!*"

She just chuckled and lay her head down and just watched everything that was going on. Buddy made his way over to us. He looked at Lily.

"I'm Buddy. I live here. I own here. I'm number one."

Lily politely lifted her head and began to answer him. "How do you do, Buddy? My name is Lily and our baby is Coconut. Thank you for sharing your lovely home with us. We will do our best to acknowledge your number one spot during our stay."

"Oh, okay, that's good. Well, you guys settle in. I'll let my mom know that I've allowed you to stay."

With that, he walked over to the middle of the room, lifted his leg and peed. I was dumbfounded and needless to say, Lily was shocked. They must have some great kind of communication, these two. Alpha Boy and mom.

"Buddy! Buddy, you bad boy!" His mom came running over with a towel to wipe it up off the floor. So much for great communication. I guess that's just Alpha talk and mom isn't really clued in on it.

She made a clean swipe and all was well. The end of the day was near and it was clearly time for dinner. With Alpha Dog running his thing, I knew we would have to steer clear of his bowl during dinner. His mom was also obviously clear on the subject of Alpha and us non-Alphas because she put his bowl in its usual place. All of our bowls were placed down only after he started eating and they were actually placed way across the room in a not-so-obvious spot. Lily and I quietly made our way to our bowls while Coconut scampered over to his and began his usual ritual of inhaling his dinner. A few times Buddy stopped eating and glanced over to look at us to make sure we weren't sneaking up on him and trying to take over his food.

There can be some very strange behavior when you bring strange animals together. We all do have our pecking orders, like most species, and respecting that order is paramount if you're going to get along. There are certain instinctive rules that abound and we all know them from inside. That's what Alpha is. Alpha is top dog, or the first guy on the list. However you want to phrase it. But since Buddy lives here and this is really his Forever Home, it would make sense that he would be Alpha Dog. Although, I overheard at the shelter that this light haired lady, who I will temporarily call Mom, brings in stray and helpless dogs all the time. Poor Buddy just might meet his match one day when one of those dogs decides that HE wants to be Alpha and poor Buddy will have to just take second spot in the line. I sure don't want to be around when that happens.

For now, I'm content to just let things be as they are. I have no desire to overtake his position although I think he just may have a run for his money with Coconut. Coconut has become a little feisty and somewhat aggressive, and I don't think that Coconut is totally inclined to accept this

Alpha Dog. And as far as his rules and regulations, well, with Coconut, he may as well be talking to that wall over there. Good luck, Alpha Boy. I'm just going to sit back and let it all play out.

After everyone was finished eating, Mom came over to us and knelt down and started petting Lily. Lily just closed her eyes and relished in the kind touch and pats on her head. Then Mom reached over to pet me. I, too, shut my eyes slightly and let her stroke me a few times. Whew, that felt good. The pressure of the last few weeks were melting away and I could feel my heart beginning to open and the lumps in my throat dissolve.

Forever Home. Forever Mom and Dad. Nice words. I took a few minutes to say a few words of thanks to Sky Dog for bringing us this far and asked if he could just hang in there with us a bit longer and help us finish the journey.

*Not a problem, JoJo.*

There he was again. Sky Dog, you are always there when we need you. You never let us down, do you?

*I'm always here, JoJo. Don't forget that. I'm always here.*

Mom got up and moved to the other side of the room and sat down to read. Lily and I nuzzled close. Thanks, Sky Dog. Thanks.

*JoJo: A Dog's Tale*

## Chapter 24

We all drifted off to sleep. Mom even fell asleep in her chair. It apparently had been a busy day for everybody and we were all glad just to be somewhat settled. As we were all waking up from our naps, there was a ringing at the door. Buddy ran to the door and started barking and barking. That was his job apparently. Mom went over to the door, opened it and in walked two new ladies. They looked very nice and gentle. I liked them immediately. Until they began to talk.

"Hi, my name is Virginia and this is Barb. We're from the Central Highlands Rescue Center. We got a call from Laura over at the animal control facility about two dogs for rescue."

"Oh, yes, please come in. Yes, their story is quite complicated, but they're all really nice dogs. I love them all. Wish I could keep them all, but, I've got a job and already have one of my own. I just take the rescues in on a temporary basis until we can find permanent homes for them."

This was it! This was going to be the day of separation for Lily and Coconut and I. Lily and I just looked at one another as she quietly came to stand by my side. Mom looked down at us.

"It's okay, guys. Don't be sad, JoJo. Lily and Coconut are going to get some really wonderful homes and you'll all be fine. These ladies are going to take Lily and Coconut today and start the hunt for their new Forever Homes."

"Oh, they are all so cute! I could just love them all to death!" One of the new ladies was cooing all over us. A lot of good it did. We were saddened immediately and the lumps in my throat were returning.

I looked at Lily. "Sweetheart, I guess this is it."

"I guess so. You be good, you hear? I know how you can get sometimes."

I chuckled. "Heh, heh, yeah, I can be a handful sometimes. Listen, I just want you to know . . . "

"Don't, JoJo. Let's not drag this out."

I nodded. We stood, we looked, we touched noses. It seemed like a cloud came over all of us and blocked out the actual leashing and picking up and walking out the door because I don't remember any of it. Suddenly, they were just gone. Gone. I turned to walk over to the wall to lay down.

"Hey, JoJo, get a grip. They're going to be fine. I've seen dozens of you guys come and go and believe me, it all works out."

It was Buddy. He was doing his best to console me, the big jerk, but I was appreciative. He walked over to me and lay down next to me and continued.

"Yeah, they come and go, but I'll tell you one thing. Everything single one that comes through here gets a perfect Forever Home. My Mom makes sure of that. Trust me, they'll be fine and you know what?"

"What?"

"You're gonna be fine, too, fella. You wait. My mom, here, is really, really good with coming up with some great Forever Homes. She's like magic in this job. It's uncanny, but she really comes up with some good ones. And I mean really, really good ones!"

My ears perked up. I was feeling a little better but I was still feeling my loss. Lily had been a great companion for many months and Coconut, well, Coconut was just Coconut. A crazy puppy kid. But if all that Buddy said was true, then we *are* all going to be fine. Yeah, I was feeling better.

"Are you feeling okay? Mom is getting ready to take me out for my daily trot. Wanna hang along? Are you up to it?"

"Sure, I'm ready. Let's go."

Mom came over and leashed us both up and out we went. As we walked down the street, I let the fresh wind embrace my nostrils. It felt good to be part of the regular world again. Buddy and I trotted side by side and seemed to bond a bit. Not totally, but I could feel his first hostility and anxiety kind of diminishing. He still carried the Alpha Dog attitude, but kept it to a minimum. I think he could feel my pain a little and didn't really want to add to my troubles and my losses so he eased off a bit. We trotted and sniffed. We peed and sniffed. We barked and sniffed. All in all, it was a good walk for both of us.

When we returned home, Mom fed us dinner and we all just hung around the house; Mom watching the big picture box and Buddy and I chewing away on a couple of toys. Then, suddenly, the little black box on her table began ringing.

"Hello?"

She had picked up a piece off the box and held it to her ear. We, of course, couldn't hear the other side of the conversation. All we could hear was what Mom was saying.

"Oh, great! Sure. Absolutely. I'll take him over first thing in the morning."

She put the piece back down on the box.

"JoJo, guess what? We've barely got you on the website and already offers are coming in to adopt you! Isn't that great? We're going over tomorrow morning to visit some people to see if we think it would be a good fit for you."

"See there? I told ya' so. Things happen fast around here." Buddy was chiming in to give me some extra info.

Should I be excited? I was having a hard time with that. I was still reeling over my loss of Lily and Coconut. I knew I would have to change my attitude really quick if I expected any new people to like me and want me. But, yes, it was hard. Perhaps a good night's sleep will make me feel better. I was sure of it.

That night after Mom went off to bed I was struggling about where to lie down to sleep. A rug here, a rug there. Nothing was making me comfortable. My thoughts ran back to the nights I used to spend in bed with Baby. Would I ever have that in my life again? I wasn't sure. In fact, I was very apprehensive. I just lay down on one of the kitchen rugs and tried to close my eyes.

Just then, standing there in the door to the kitchen, was Buddy.

"Hey, listen. I've got this really, really big bed in here in the living room. Uh, if you like, I mean if it would be more comfortable, I'd like to invite you over to share it with me."

I didn't say anything. I just looked at him. Gratefully. I got up and followed him into the living room and just like he said, there was this really huge doggie bed. He stepped in and turned around. Then he just lay down. I stepped in, turned around a few times and picked a small spot on the other side of the bed. It felt good. The bed felt good. And the invitation felt good.

" 'Night."

"Good night," I managed to squeek out.

"Things will be good, my friend."

"Thanks, Buddy. You're a real buddy."

"Heh,heh. The guy's a comedian."

*JoJo: A Dog's Tale*

## Chapter 25

The next morning I was more apprehensive than ever. Mom was in the kitchen scurrying around to get us and her fed before we scooted out the door. My mind was reeling with questions and my stomach was a mess.

"Listen, Buddy, what if I don't like these people? What if I don't like the place? What if the vibes are bad?"

"Hey, you've got a mouth. Use it. Just bark like crazy. Keep running for the door. Nip at ankles. Pee if you have to. Just let Mom know. She is really good at picking up the signs. She's real sensitive to us and how we're feeling."

"Really?"

"Really. If you hate the place or the people, just let her know. She'll get it."

I thought that the concept was good, but I sure wish I could do a practice run. But no such luck. Mom was reaching for her coat and I was on the leash quicker than you can say doggie biscuit!

The whole trip over I could hear my stomach doing flip-flops, but I decided to brave it and really try to give this whole thing a chance. We arrived, Mom parked the car and off we went to the front door. She rang the bell and it took several minutes for someone to come and open the door.

Finally, the door opened and there stood this rather nasty looking kid. He grabbed for me right away. I barked and growled.

"Hey! Don't do that! I'll bite you right back, you stinker!"

Okay, this was not a good start. Right away I'm hating this kid and I'm not liking the smell of the place and the vibes were questionable.

"Well, well, what do we have here?"

There was this rather stout woman standing in the kitchen looking down at me. Didn't like her either. And the vibes were getting really bad.

"Hi, I'm Sandi from the United Yorkie Rescue. We understand that you're interested in adopting."

"Yes, my little boy here has been pestering me for months about getting a dog, but I'm not sure he's up to the task of taking care of a dog. But I thought if I adopted from a shelter or some such place rather than spend hundreds of dollars on a pedigree, I won't be out too much money if we have to get rid of it down the line."

Okay, another red flag. I sure hope Mom is listening to all this. I decided to take Buddy's advice and I started in with my best bark and growl. The kid came closer again and I growled worse and really went for his ankles. Then, I decided to clinch the deal. I walked over to the living room carpet, lifted my leg, and... well, you know the rest.

"Oh, Jesus, get that thing off my carpet!"

With that, Mom came over, picked me up and simply said, "Well, actually, I don't think you folks are really ready for a dog. Perhaps when your son is a little older might be better."

Well, Buddy was right. Mom sure knew her business. We were out of there in ten minutes flat and on our way home. I sat in the car seat with, I'm sure, a very smug look on my face. Mom just started the car and looked over.

"Okay, little fella, I get the picture. You are not going to be shy about letting me know what's going to be good for you and what isn't. Hang in there, there's somebody perfect out there for you. There is a place for you and we're going to find it!"

I smiled my dog smile and off we went. I like this lady. I wish I could stay with her, but it is not to be. But I'm banking on what she and Buddy keep telling me. That somewhere there's a place for me. Actually, I know there's a place for me. I'm feeling it in my bones.

We made about four or five more of these little futile trips to potential Forever Homes. None, and I mean, none of them were for me. There was either too many kids, the people were too old, the vibes stunk. You name it. But nothing fit.

I don't know how many darks I had been with this Mom, but it seemed like there was a really long time since our last visit to a home. It was like no one was asking about me any more. No one was calling. No one seemed to want me. Then one day, Mom was sitting at her click box, the one with the big picture in front of it. She started to tap, tap away at the finger board and she seemed to be real excited.

"Oh my goodness, would you look at this, JoJo? Here's someone that just might be a perfect fit for you!"

She kept tapping away at the finger board. "Listen to this. Here's a lady that lives pretty close, has no kids, doesn't work any more, has a big back yard, has a pool that her and her husband use all the time, loves little dogs, has a big house, AND .. AND are you ready for this? Would let a new little puppy sleep in bed with them? How's that for perfect?"

Wow! Wowee wow! Is she for real? I'm feelin' it! I'm feelin' this one!

"She says she's been looking at your picture for ten days. Every day something kept pulling her back to your picture!"

This is it! This is the one! That's why nobody has been calling for me! Oh gosh, can it be true?

"Hey, kid, it's me, Big Dog. Listen, you better be gettin' ready. We've been workin' this one out fer ya'. Whaddaya think of that?"

"*Big Dog?!* Is that really you? Oh god, can it be true? Is this really going to happen?"

"Hey, this one's a real corker, kiddo. This is the big one. Get ready!"

I felt a trickle down my leg. Don't tell me. I was so embarrassed. But I was beside myself with joy. This is unbelievable!

"Yeah, we haven't let anybody get to you and we've been pushing this lady every day to connect with you. She's perfect, kiddo, and she loves, loves, loves animals!"

"Oh, Big Dog, this is just too perfect. Thank you! Thank you!"

I was starting to pant and pace. Just then, Buddy came walking in.

"What is up with you, Prancy Pants?"

I told him the whole story.

"See? Told ya' my Mom would get it together for you? Looks like you're feeling this one already."

"Oh, Buddy, I can feel this one all the way to the tips of my fur. This is the one, I know it! This is the one."

"Well, if you're feeling it that much, then you're right. This probably is the one. Hey, good luck!"

"Thanks! Thanks, Buddy! I can hardly stand it. I think she said we're going to visit in three darks. I will not sleep, you know that."

"Well, whatever. Maybe when Mom takes us out we can use a lot of our energy to get you tired so you can sleep. I'll help you."

"Thanks, Buddy. You truly are a buddy!"

"Oh, stop that!"

The next three days were hell. I paced during the day. I slept hour by hour at night, waking at every hour to check where the moon was and how long it would be for the dark to be over so we could start the next day. I waited and waited.

Finally, the day had come. We all got up early and Mom scooped me up and out we went. First stop, bath and haircut. Yikes! Who knew. I guess that's what you have to do to make a good impression. And good impression was on the top of my list today. Normally, bath and haircut would not be a favorite of mine, but if it meant making a good impression, well, lather me up!

I knew one thing for sure. I was glad that Lily and Coconut weren't here to see this. They would think I was totally nuts by now. But a good nuts.

As I was being frothed and rinsed, my mind wandered. Could it be? Would it be? Is this really the day? My heart skipped a beat. I prayed.

*Sky Dog, are you with me?*
*I'm here, JoJo, I'm here.*
*Make this happen, Sky Dog, make this happen!*
I held my breath. I waited.
He didn't answer.

## Chapter 26

The drive to the new visit and new Mom felt like it was excruciatingly long. I sat and sat and sat, my heart pounding, my fur curling in spite of the new wash. What should I do? How should I act? I realized I should have spoken with Buddy to get some tips from him. He sure knew what to do to get OUT of a place but now I needed to know how to get IN to a place.

I decided that I would just be myself and just try and look cute. But I ran a phrase through my head over and over again. *Don't pee. Don't pee. Don't pee.* I was determined to be the best of the best.

We turned a corner and drove up a drive. There in front of us was this beautiful house. All pearly looking and bright. Lots of trees and bushes all over and nice things in the windows. Mom got out and came over to my side to get me out of the car seat. She leashed me and put me down and we walked up the walk to the front door. She rang the bell. The doorbell sounded like a symphony from heaven! The music was so long and beautiful I could hardly stand it. And then it happened! The door opened.

Standing there before me was the most beautiful, light-haired smiling lady I had ever seen. She started talking and her voice sounded like an angel, all singy songy and warm. We stepped inside. The smells! Oh my gosh, the smells! There was food and flowers and beautiful aromas from everywhere. Even the new lady smelled good. I just stood there. She started talking.

"Oh my goodness, would you look at this precious little guy? Oh, he is just the best! Take his leash off."

"But he'll run all over the house, including upstairs."

"Well, if he's going to live here, he's going to be running all over anyway."

"But he might pee."

"We'll get over it."

Music to my ears! Mom took my leash off and I began to run around and sniff, sniff, sniff. Everything smelled so good. And the vibes! The vibes were unbelievable! Love! So much love in this house. I could hardly contain myself.

Mom and New Mom sat down to talk while I continued to scamper all over. I couldn't get enough. I wanted to smell everything. I wanted to put my nose on everything. I wanted to be a part of everything. Then I stopped. Oh, oh. What if . . . I wasn't going to think about it. I just kept moving.

Finally, I was tuckered out. I just stood next to Mom looking at New Mom. I looked into her eyes and she looked right back. Right then, I knew. I knew this was it. I slowly walked over to her and lifted myself up so my paws touched her leg and I was leaning on her. She reached down to pick me up. She held me like she had been holding me all my life. She knew exactly how and where to hold me.

She reached over to a cup and took a dab of something with her finger and held it to my nose. It was peanut butter! I remembered peanut butter from when Baby use to give me some dabs from her sandwich. I loved it then and I still loved it. How did New Mom know?

I licked it off her hands as she smiled this warm, beautiful smile with her eyes twinkling. This was going to be the moment. This was going to be the signal. I softly licked her cheek and then softly licked the tip of her nose.

Other Mom said, "Oh my goodness. I think we have a match. He always lets me know when it's a good visit or a bad visit. So far, they've all been bad except this one. Yes, we definitely have a match."

I kept looking at New Mom and she kept looking at me. Then she kissed my nose. I thought I would melt like butter in the sun. I took the deepest breath of my life and sighed the biggest sigh of my life and just nestled into her arms. I knew I wasn't going anywhere.

I knew this was the dream of all dreams come true. I knew this was truly my Forever Home!

The house, the smells, the vibes, the eyes, the smiles, the hugs, the kisses. It just wasn't going to get any better than this. I felt the water again in the corner of my eye. It was okay. I felt a lump in my throat again. It was okay. But the best part, I felt the warmth of her arms around me and the security of those arms. It was better than okay. It was perfect!

# Chapter 27

It has been many, many darks that I've been with my new Forever Mom and Dad. I met Dad shortly after that first day and it was kind of different for me. Since my first experience, I was kind of wary of most men, but this new Dad, well, he is like no other man I've ever known. He loves me! How do I know?

The way he treats me and the way he talks to me. The way he holds me and the way he plays with me. And he, too, has loads and loads of love in his eyes. Yeah, my Dad and I are a team. He has totally accepted that I've taken over as Alpha Dog and doesn't even give me any arguments about it.

And yeah, I sleep in bed with them. How cool is that? That was a big issue with me. I feel so safe and secure when I'm in bed with them.

Let me just tell you a little bit about my life here with my Forever Mom and my Forever Dad. They have given me everything I could possibly want or need. I have the best food, the best toys, the best clothes (ugh).

They have a big pool and I have my own special pool float with a canopy. I especially love the pool because I love to lounge and I feel like a king out there.

It's almost a sacred spot and I am a very happy dog when I'm out there.

I have a car seat and a carrier. Sometimes when we go on trips, they have a carrier that Dad wears on his chest and they put me in it and we all go shopping. I also have a doggie stroller. AND . . we go for soft and creamy! (ice cream) But the best part of my day is my rest time. I was always too scared in all the other places to really rest.

And I am never afraid here. I know they will take care of me. They have pledged themselves to me and I know that I AM THEIR DOG! If all of us were their dog, there would be no problems in the world.

Well, you've read my story and you've traveled my journey with me. I hope you've also experienced the emotions that have surged through my veins during each and every incident. Yes, we do have emotions. And we do have feelings. I can be hurt emotionally. I can be scared. I can be any emotion that you can be. I love. I cry. I fear.

Know that every animal has more than feelings. They have a soul just like humans. Not the same as humans and actually sometimes more. Animals are every bit as important as humans and it's important that humans understand.

My biggest dream was to just find someone who would love me as much as I was willing to love them. You see, that's what we do. We love. Unconditionally. And all of us are just jam-packed with it and we are willing to give it every day over and over and over again. What is so hard about simply asking to be loved in return? Yes, we have a soul and we have a right to be here. And we are one and the same when it comes to love, you and I.

The next time you think about giving up a pet, consider the emotions that pet is going to suffer. After your pet has lived with you for so long and loved you unconditionally day after day, you drop them off at a shelter, or worse, just somewhere in a field. They feel loss. They feel abandonment. They feel fear. They feel uncertainty. And the list goes on.

You can look in their eyes and simply see the emotions that are there every day. We smile. We laugh. We wonder. We question. We ache.

But that's the best of scenarios. Let's talk a minute about those humans out there that physically abuse us. If we could stand up against you, I'm not so sure that we would even do that. You see, our love abounds. And through all the physical pain, we're still hoping that somewhere in there is just a speck of love from you and after it's all over, you'll pick us up and hug us forever. When that doesn't happen, we cry, we ache, we yearn.

How about those puppy mills? Over my travels, I've learned a lot about them and let me tell you, my heart breaks every time I think about them. Some of those poor dogs never touch the ground. Never see the sky. Never smell fresh air. They are crippled from poor diets or cramped conditions. Their fur is matted and their nails are overgrown and curled. Doesn't that just make your stomach turn? It does mine.

I can tell you that I pray to Sky Dog every night that all the humans of the world will somehow be touched by some magical light and ALL the humans' hearts will open up and they will all become like my Mom and Dad. Or like the lady that took me in. Or the thousands of others out there who are scrambling the globe to save us. Just know, you lovely humans, that we know what you're doing and we cannot even describe the love that flows from us for all that you do.

Yes, we have feelings. Unfortunately, what we don't have is control over our own destiny. That's why we need you. We rely on you.

My hope from this writing is that the message gets out there to everyone. My story had a good ending. I went from horrible to happy, and what a happy it is! I am so attached to my Forever Mom and Dad that I almost get hysterical if they leave my sight. But you know what? They know that and they do everything in their power to keep me close. They know my feelings. They know my fears. They hug and kiss me every morning and carry me around the house and they do everything in their power to make my fears go away.

They call me the Prince. And I feel like a Prince. Each day, my security level gets stronger and stronger. Each day my past fears diminish a little more. Each day I get more and more hugs and kisses! I still have memories of my other life and memories of Lily and Coconut. I talked with Lily not too long ago and she is very, very happy as is Coconut, who, I hear, is more spoiled than I am, if that's possible.

Understand that the only thing that we have is hope. Hope that we'll find that great Forever Mom and Dad and Forever Home. Hope that we'll be loved with as much fervor as we're willing to give. Hope that we will be released from the cages and lifted up into someone's loving arms. But some poor animals don't even have that because they've never been given a fair chance for a decent life.

You must understand the most important thing that I'm trying to tell you. And that is, we love YOU! We're all trying to love you unconditionally. We're all trying to make your lives happy and filled. All we ask is that you love us in return. And loving is caring, caring for your animal as though they were your child. That animals need the same kind of care, love and attention. We are little beings, also.

Please care for us. Please love us. Make the horrible go away and bring us happy.

May Sky Dog bless you over and over for just reading my story and understanding my message. If you spread the word, maybe, just maybe we can all get along and love one another Forever. It is everything a dog could hope for.

If we don't understand the meaning of love between all of our species, I'm afraid the Earth will not survive. It is love that makes the world go round, keeps it together, and keeps it alive. Even with all the troubles of the world, love is what snaps it all back together. Yes, love truly is the answer.

Well, thanks for listening, but I gotta go. Dad's calling me for soft and creamy! Now that's what I call love.

*JoJo: A Dog's Tale*

*JoJo: A Dog's Tale*

## Dr. Kim Ogden, Dr.P.H.
## Bibliography

In the interest of accuracy and clarification, we have included a bibliography of Dr. Kim Ogden's participation regarding JoJo's story. Following are facts and statements and information received directly from JoJo through Dr. Kim's animal communication expertise. This information is included in the story along with other details of the story that have been created for the purposes of entertainment only.

**Session No. 1:**
1. Will you talk with Dr. Kim?
"I know all about the book. Ask me anything. I have a lot to say. I knew I would be talking with this new person." (Dr. Kim says JoJo talks like a New Yorker.)
2. "What's happening with my eyes? I get 'guck' in my eyes." (Mom and Dad clean his eyes with pads with a solution. We call them 'eye guckies'. Dr. Kim did not know this.) He came up with his own solution for Mom to use her fingers instead and do it every day.
3. Doesn't like being called Boo Boo. He wants to be called JoJo. (Mom explained that Boo or Boo Boo is a term of endearment.)
4. Quite upset when discussing first family. Big burp!
5. Doesn't want the book to be about "Poor JoJo." Wants it to be "Yeah, JoJo!" We discuss this later on.
6. Husband or male figure from first family is not okay with him. He refers to a "smell" that we are assuming is alcohol. Once when the smell was present, JoJo was kicked in the

head. He is sensitive around his anal area. This is from being picked up by his tail and hung overhead. Mom responded to JoJo, "I am so sorry this happened to you and I can promise it will never, ever happen again. Not as long as you're in this house!"

7. JoJo asked what he is going to get out of all this "book business?" We asked what he wanted and he said "soft and creamy" three times a day. Soft and creamy is ice cream that he gets every night in bed with Mom. (Dr. Kim did not know this.) We said once a day is good for health reasons.

8. We said good-bye for now.

**Session No. 2**

1. JoJo still wants to make sure that the book is not all about tears. He wants a lot of happy. Mom promised that there would be a lot of hope and JoJo being positive about his future throughout the ordeal. He said this was good.

2. He loved Lily. He grieves for Lily and Coconut.

3. JoJo remembers being "stashed away" someplace. His eyes hurt and is sorry for Lily feeling so hot. Breathing was more of a problem than lack of food, but then food and water became a big problem. They kept wondering when someone was going to come for them. It took many, many days for that to happen.

4. Then they moved around to many places with lots and lots of cages. Life was not all that good before, but they never expected this to happen to them.

5. The man who took them to the vet and the shelter were their "savior." It was a terrible time. All of them almost died.

6. "But I want all dogs to know that it CAN go from horrible to happy."
7. "That's all for now," he says.

### Session No. 3
1. JoJo is tired today. Doesn't feel much like talking. (JoJo had a nail clipping appointment the prior day and he always needs a tranquilizer for this because it is huge trauma for him. Today he is still feeling the effects of the tranquilizer. Dr. Kim did not know this.)
2. Mom and Dad and JoJo are leaving on a 10-day trip. He says he knows that. Wants to know if he will be able to potty on the way. Mom says yes.
3. We discussed using crates in motel rooms when Mom and Dad go out for dinner. He said, "Please, no crates!" But says he loves hot dogs if we could please do that for him along the way. (He does love hot dogs! Dr. Kim did not know that.)
4. We talked about how exciting and interesting the trip is going to be and he will see a lot of new things. He says "I've seen enough things!" He says he is going for us.

### Session No. 4
1. We have returned from trip. JoJo says he is exhausted and would have rather stayed home. He says, "We just kept going and going and going. I wanted to just land somewhere!" He said he never knew where he was going but was confident that Mom and Dad were not going to leave him anywhere.

## JoJo: A Dog's Tale

2. Didn't like all the new rooms. Too many smells. (We are assuming he's talking about the motel rooms we stayed in every night.)

3. Being adopted by Mom and Dad is the best thing that could ever happen to a dog. We asked if there was anything more we could do to make him happier. He said, "To not go to so many places!" (Again, the trip.)

4. He loves the swimming pool at the house. Feels like a king when he lounges there. Feels like a 'sacred,' happy dog. (A few days earlier, we had him in his pool float with the canopy. He had his paws on the edge looking out as he floated across the pool. I said he looked like a pharaoh in his 'sacred' barge. Dr. Kim did not know that.)

5. The best part of his days is when he can just rest. He says he was not able to do that in other places because he was either too scared or too worried.

6. He says he is never afraid with his Mom and Dad. He says he is THEIR dog. He knows they will take care of him and they have pledged themselves to him.

Final words from JoJo are in the last chapter and are almost verbatim as they came across from him to Dr. Kim. He is very concerned about the future of Earth and the connection between humans and animals that, he says, must be made in order to survive. He also says that other dogs should have a chance to tell their stories and that this is just the beginning. He thanks his Mom for everything she has done for him and his hope is that all humans, some day, could gain the same understanding. It is everything a dog could hope for.

*JoJo: A Dog's Tale*

*JoJo: A Dog's Tale*